D1248061

DIVORCE AND REMARRIAGE IN THE EARLY CHURCH

A History of Divorce and Remarriage in the Ante-Nicene Church

DIVORCE AND REMARRIAGE IN THE EARLY CHURCH

A History of Divorce and Remarriage in the Ante-Nicene Church

by

Pat Edwin Harrell

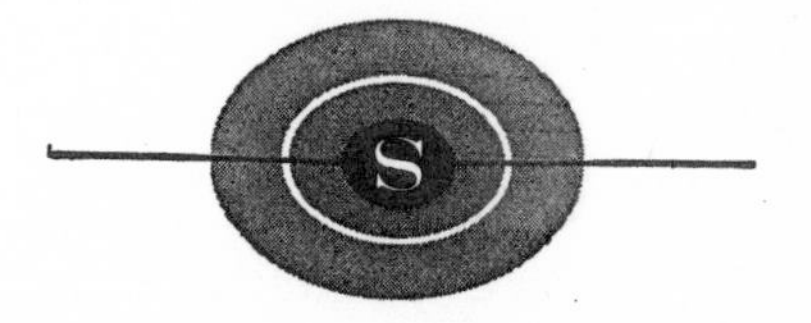

R. B. Sweet Company, Inc.
Austin, Texas 78751

To

M. D. W.

ACKNOWLEDGMENTS

The original manuscript, in a slightly different form, was presented to the Faculty of the Boston University School of Theology as a partial fulfillment of the requirements for the Doctor of Theology degree.

My indebtedness to my advisors, Dr. Edwin Prince Booth, Dr. Richard M. Cameron, and especially Dr. Harrell Beck, who although acknowledged, cannot be repaid.

Appreciation for the patience of the Church of Christ in Natick, Massachusetts, where the author served as Minister during the preparation of the manuscript, is gratefully acknowledged.

CONTENTS

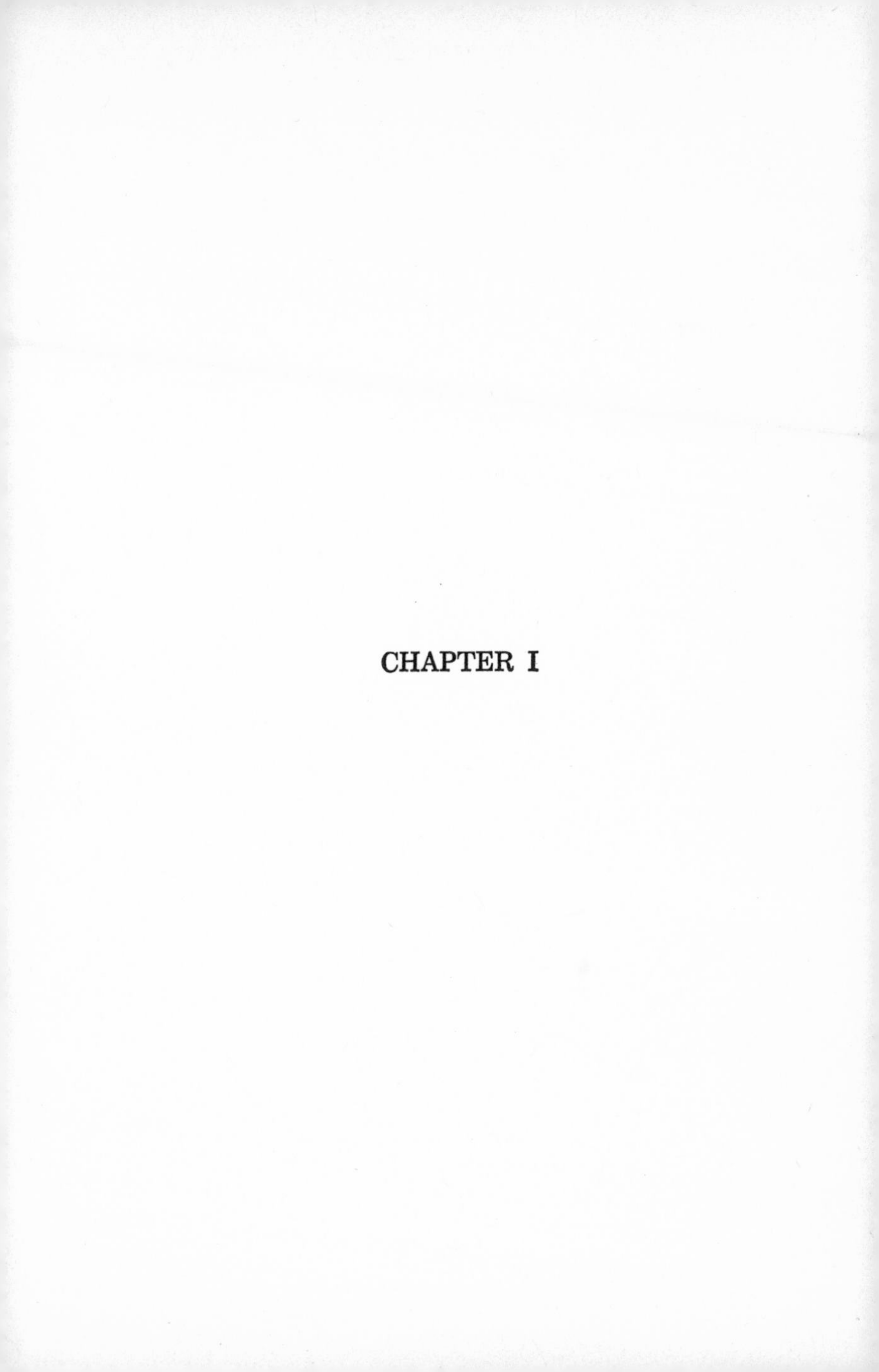

CHAPTER I

THE ENIGMA OF DIVORCE AND REMARRIAGE

Divorce and remarriage is a frequent phenomenon in our society, and this has proved to be something of an enigma to the church. What should the church's attitude be toward those who have been divorced and remarried? Are they to be pitied or reproved, disciplined or tolerated? On what basis should ecclesiastical policy be determined? The answers to these questions have varied, ranging from the extremes of unbending legalism to apparent indifference. These attitudes exist not only between denominations, but are also found within most communions.

THE PROBLEM

The problem of divorce and remarriage ceases to be academic and becomes acute when a church member divorces and remarries or when a divorced person presents himself for the church membership. It is always a grave matter for missionaries serving in polygamous lands. For guidance toward a solution to the problem, the church has often looked back to the historic roots of the faith, that is, to the Apostolic and early church. There has not been, however, unanimity among scholars as to the position of the first Christians, and consequently the matter of divorce and remarriage remains an enigma for the church.

Statement of Purpose

While many studies have been made on the early church's attitude toward divorce and remarriage, unfortunately, most investigations have been concerned with only a portion of the problem. There are two basic questions, as indicated by the problems confronting a contemporary church, which must be dealt with separately. These are: (1) what was the attitude of the early church toward Christians who were divorced and remarried? and (2) what was the attitude of the early church toward catechumens who were divorced and remarried? Neither facet can be clearly seen alone; they can only be viewed in proper perspective when considered together. It is the purpose of this study, therefore, to ascertain the attitude of the Ante-Nicene Church toward the divorce and remarriage of both members and catechumens. The conclusions of this study will not themselves solve the enigma of divorce in the modern church, that must remain for the theologians, but they will clarify the historic position to which these scholars have appealed.

Definition of Terms

Ante-Nicene Church.—The Ante-Nicene Church is interpreted as the organized Christian movement from its beginning on Pentecost through the Council of Nicea in A.D. 325.

Divorce.—Divorce is viewed as the formal, legal severance of the marital union. It includes the right of remarriage, whether or not the right is exercised, and is not merely the separation from bed and board.

Christian.—Throughout this study Christian is understood to mean an individual who has identified himself with the church through baptism and an acceptance of church discipline.

Catechumen.—A catechumen is regarded as one who is sympathetic to Christianity and who contemplates church membership. The word is employed without reference to his actually being engaged in a formal instructional program.

Methodology

Approach.—The attitude of the Ante-Nicene Church toward divorce and remarriage is to be ascertained through a historical and not a theological approach. There have been investigations which have treated it as basically a theological problem; that is, on the basis of theology it is decided what the position of the Ante-Nicene Church probably was, and in the light of that decision the historical material is interpreted. The approach of this study will be to survey the primary sources to see what was the practice of the Ante-Nicene Church and then to attempt to ascertain the theological position behind the practice. The beliefs of the church during this period can only be understood by looking at the interaction of the attitude of divorce and remarriage in Jewish and Roman society and morality in general with ideals of Christians who lived in the world, but were not of the world. Attention will be given, therefore, to marriage, divorce, and sexual morality in the Roman and Jewish worlds, in the New Testament, and finally in the Ante-Nicene Church.

Scope.—The Ante-Nicene Church, unlike Melchizedek, had predecessors and successors which are not without significance. It is obvious that the ministry of Jesus, which was before this period, is not only significant, but also crucial. Upon his teaching the doctrine of the Ante-Nicene Church was presumably based. Likewise, there are some references after the Council of Nicea which reflect either a crystallization of trends beginning within the period of investigation, or the emergence of new views contrary to the Ante-Nicene position. When these trends are cited, specific contention is made that they belong to the Post-Nicene period.

Limitation.—There is a vast amount of material in the period under investigation that deals with marriage in general. This study will be limited to those aspects of marriage that pertain to its permanency.

LITERATURE

The problem of divorce and remarriage in Christianity has not been ignored by scholars. There is a vast corpus of literature on the subject, especially on the New Testament doctrine. Much of what has been written, however, is polemic and dogmatic in nature, or else is merely a repetition of what has already been said on the subject. The material focuses around the question of the permanency of matrimony. Neither the view of marriage as indissoluble or dissoluble has lacked able and learned advocates. The focal point also represents theological positions, with the indissoluble view being championed by Roman Catholics and many Anglicans, while the more lenient position is held by Protestant bodies in general.

The literature as a whole has one or more of the following flaws: (1) an attempt to understand the New Testament doctrine without a grasp of the Jewish-Roman background, or the Ante-Nicene Church's interpretation of that doctrine; (2) a lack of familiarity with recent Roman Catholic interpretations of the "exception clauses" of the first Gospel; (3) a theological commitment to a position before the investigation has been made. It is the purpose of this book to supplement the previous treatments in these three respects.

CHAPTER II

THE BACKGROUND OF HELLENISTIC MARRIAGE

Christianity arose in that fringe of civilization around the Mediterranean Sea dominated by the Roman Empire. Although Jewish in origin, Christianity became almost exclusively a Gentile movement after the destruction of the Jewish Temple by Titus.[1] The Hellenistic attitude toward marriage and divorce and morality in general is important, therefore, because Christianity drew many of its converts from Hellenistic society. The attitude in the Roman world toward marriage and divorce is amply illustrated in the writings of the lawyers, dramatists, historians, and moralists. It is, of course, impossible to date with precision moral sentiments. It is apparent, however, that the moral situation during the first three Christian centuries had its beginning before the coming of Christ. This chapter will be concerned in general with the condition in the centuries before the beginning of Christianity, more specifically with the situation from the consulship of Sextus Aelius Paetus, the first to compile a book of Roman law (198 B.C.), to the reign of Constantine, the first Christian Emperor (323 A.D.).

MARRIAGE

Long before the rise of the Empire, Roman society was monogamous.[2] From the earliest times these unions could take one of several forms. The jurist Gaius (A.D. 200) lists them as: "*usus*, *confarreatio*, and *coemptio*."[3] The important feature of these different forms is that they all involve the concept of *manus*, that is, the wife passed from the authority of her father into the hand of her husband who exercised over her absolute power.[4]

Marriages with manus.—The most solemn form of marriage was the *confarreatio*. This was a ceremony involving a religious sacrifice and the presence of ten witnesses. In speaking of the *far*, a grain used in sacrifice at the ceremony, Dionysius commented upon the union in the following words:

> From the sharing of *far* was named the ceremony whereby wives share with their husbands the earliest and most holy food, and agree to share their fortune in life too; it brought them into a close bond of indissoluble relationship, and nothing could break a marriage of that kind. This law directed wives to live so as to please their husbands only, as they had nowhere else to appeal, and husbands to govern their wives as things which were necessary to them and inalienable.[5]

The laws governing this type of union were attributed to Romulus.[6] By the end of the Republic this form of marriage had fallen into disuse and was rare during the

Empire. The difficulty Tiberius had in finding someone qualified for the priesthood of Jupiter, a prerequisite of which was to have been born of a *confarreatio* union, is related by Tacitus[7] and is evidence of its rarity.

The *coemptio* was a fictitious sale of the bride by the father.[8] In nature it was similar to the transfer of property, although strictly speaking she was not treated as chattel.[9] Jurists writing after the time of Gaius fail to mention *coemptio*; this form of marriage was probably rare before he compiled the *Institutes*.[10]

The third form of marriage was the *usus*. After a year of cohabitation, provided the woman was not absent for three successive nights, the union was recognized as a legal marriage.[11] Gaius wrote that this was in "part abolished by mere disuse."[12] Like the other two types of marriage with *manus, usus* probably disappeared before the beginning of the Empire.[13]

Marriage without manus.—In the declining years of the Republic the forms of marriage with *manus* declined because of the dissolvement of the concept of *pater familias*.[14] In the place of unions involving the unpopular *manus* there developed free unions based on mutual consent. This was practically the only type of marriage during the Empire.[15]

Depreciation of Marriage

Both philosophy and religion combined to depreciate marriage in Roman society. These forces resulted in the restriction, and in some cases, the discouragement of matrimony.

Abstinence.—There was shortly before the rise of Christianity a growing concern for asceticism. Undoubtedly many factors contributed to this sentiment. The Stoic morality exercised a great influence. Epictetus, a representative of the Stoa, extolls the ideal Cynic who remains unmarried.[16] The Stoic idea is well represented in the writings of Seneca. After quoting a reply from Panaetius, Seneca comments:

> That was Panaetius' answer to the man who asked him about love. I apply it to all emotions. Let us keep back, as far as we can, from slippery places; even on dry grounds we do not stand too steadily.[17]

The philosophy of Pythagoreanism and Neoplatonism contributed to the ascetic tendency.[18] The latter was influential after the beginning of the Christian era in the personage of Plotinus (c.A.D. 250). He felt that "to lapse into carnal love is a sin."[19] To him the soul must rise upward from the physical nature. This he calls "a natural impulse towards the natural terminus of marriage."[20] Additional contributions were made by the religion of Isis and other dualistic cults in their emphasis on a "stringent bodily abstinence."[21] Two brief passages suffice to show this factor working in the worship of Isis. The poet Tibullus laments:

> What help to me is Isis, or the cymbals, Delia, so often beaten by your hand? all your retreats and all your pure ablutions, and ritual nights spent in a

lonely bed?[22]

The Isis attitude is reflected also by Ovid who advises a mistress to increase her lover's ardour by continence. "Often refuse a night. Call it a headache; and Isis sometimes makes a good excuse."[23] Although these authors have distorted the principle of abstinence to serve sensuality, they reflect the association of abstinence with the worship of Isis. The ascetic spirit gained such a sway that finally Augustus attempted to correct it through legislation. His course of action, however, was not an innovation. As early as 403 B.C., according to Valerius Maximus,[24] there was a censorial decree against celibacy. Similarly Gellius[25] records a speech of the censor Merellus on the subject and goes on to say that "the state cannot be safe unless marriages are frequent."[26] It was Augustus, however, who went to the greatest lengths to check celibacy. During the time from 18 B.C. to A.D. 9 a series of laws was adopted which collectively were called the *Julia rogationes*, and contained the *lex sumptuaria*, the *lex Julia de adulteriis pudicitia*, the *lex Julia de maritandis ordinibus*, and the *lex Papia Poppaea*. There are numerous references to the legislation in the literature of that time. Suetonius,[27] Cassius Dio,[28] and the *Digesta*[29] speak of the opposition to the laws which Augustus rigidly enforced. Tacitus tells of the fear of spies in every household.[30] The device which Augustus employed was to liberalize the rights of women with children and prohibit the childless and unmarried from taking property under a will.[31]

Second Marriages.—Along with the movement toward asceticism and abstinence, there was a tendency to hold in high regard one who did not remarry after his mate's death. Thus a frequent epithet occurring on the tombs was that of *univirae*.[32] The rationale for this practice according to the lines Virgil gives Dido,[33] was that a wife's affection for her husband was so profound that it did not cease with death. When men abstained from a second marriage, the motive most often was a concern for their children. Since children born to a concubine were not legitimate and could not prejudice the claims of the children born in wedlock, there was a preference for concubinage over second marriages. Illegitimate children had no claim upon the estate whereas those of a second marriage did.[34] It was also doubted whether a stepmother could best serve the interest of the children of the first marriage. An ancient law excluded from the council any man who was so unconcerned about his children as to bring a stepmother into the house.[35] Marcus Aurelius, according to his biographer, preferred to take a concubine rather than remarry.[36] The custom of marrying only once is extolled as a virtue of the Germans by Tacitus.[37] And this romantic approach is perhaps best expressed by Statius. In lamenting the passing of his wife he said, "To love a wife when living is a pleasure; to love her when dead is an act of religion."[38]

DIVORCE

Marriage was, of course, terminated by death, and many preferred not to remarry. It could also be terminated by divorce. Although divorce was always possible in Roman society, according to a common tradition, there were no divorces for 500 years.[39] In those marriages involving *manus*, the husband could simply repudiate his wife since she was under his absolute power. The wife had no corresponding privilege. In free marriages either party could obtain a divorce. Gradually this privilege permitted to women in the free unions was also extended to *manus* marriages.[40] By the Christian era divorce was a possible means of terminating every marriage.

Grounds for Divorce

Divorce was possible, according to tradition attributed to the days of Romulus, on grounds of adultery and for wine drinking on the part of the wife.[41] Plutarch records that the use of poison and the substitution of children were valid grounds.[42] Divorce for grounds other than these entailed the husband forfeiting his property; half went to his wife and half to Ceres.[43] How diligently this early law was enforced is questionable. The grounds for divorce were soon expanded to include "perverse and disgusting conduct."[44] Suspicious Gallus repudiated his wife because she had gone out without her veil.[45] The wife of Antistius Vetus was divorced because she was observed speaking with a freedman of doubtful reputation.[46] Amilius Paulus put away his wife without specifying the grounds. When surprise was expressed that such an apparently ideal wife was repudiated, Paulus replied that only the owner knows where a new pair of shoes pinches.[47] Cicero divorced his wife of many years simply on the grounds that he wanted to improve his financial position by a union with a wealthy woman.[48] Men were not the only ones who availed themselves of an easy divorce. Cicero reports the case of a woman divorcing her husband without a pretext on the day that he returned from his province.[49]

Frequency of Divorce

The infrequency of divorce in early times must not be taken as an indication of morality. As Kiefer warns, the husband could not commit misconduct since he had absolute power.[50] But divorce gradually became more common until Cicero's time, judging from the references in literature, when it was the accepted practice. Pompey was twice widowed and twice divorced.[51] Cicero was twice divorced.[52] His wife, Terentia, amply consoled herself by marrying twice after she had been divorced by Cicero.[53] Cato remarried his divorced wife after a subsequent marriage had left her wealthy.[54] Perhaps the best evidence as to the frequency of divorce, however, is the legislation of Augustus. His concern was not with divorce *per se*, but the effect divorce had on the declining birth rate.[55]

Legislation is hardly enacted unless needed. The frequency of divorce which called forth laws also provided fruitful material for the satirists. A certain Telesilla who had married ten husbands is called by Martial an "adulteress by form of law."[56] Juvenal speaks of a woman "wearing out her bridal veil" as she flees from one home to another. In the course of five autumns, he reports, she had eight husbands.[57] Seneca scornfully writes of the lack of shame on the public's part concerning frequent dissolutions of marriage.

> Is there any woman that blushes at divorce now that certain illustrious and noble ladies reckon their years, not by the number of consuls, but by the number of their husbands, and leave home in order to marry, and marry in order to be divorced?[58]

He further remarks that divorce was so common that "every gazette has a divorce case."[59]

Restraint of Divorce

The more solemn a marriage, the more difficult it was to secure a divorce. Marriage by *confarreatio* required a similar religious ceremony to dissolve the union.[60] In marriages of *coemptio* and *usus* the divorce was an emancipation just as a *paterfamilias* might emancipate a child.[61] At first there were no laws or customs which regulated the free unions since they could be terminated by an informal act. The words of repudiation apparently varied, but obviously some formula was in use. Juvenal's description of the love Sartorius had for Bibula indicated it was simple.

> Let three wrinkles make their appearance; let her skin become dry and flabby . . . then will his freedman give her the order, "Pack up your traps and be off, and quick about it."[62]

Under Augustus, statements of repudiation were required to be made in the presence of seven witnesses.

The most effective preventive of divorce was the requirement concerning the *dos* or the gift of property made to the husband by the wife.[63] In the event that the union was terminated by a divorce, the wife had the right to reclaim the *dos*. A portion of the *dos* was forfeited if the wife were the guilty party. The law, according to the jurist Ulpian,[64] was that a sixth was kept back for immorality and an eighth for offenses of a lighter nature. When the husband was the offender, he was required to restore the *dos* at once if the cause of the divorce was immorality. If it was for a lesser offense, he could repay it by biannual installments. Augustus, in his legislation, strengthened the right of the woman to reclaim the *dos* which would make her available for another union.[65] The inadequacy of his legislation to correct the situation is indicated by the fact that similar laws had to be enacted by Domitian[66] and Septimius Severus.[67]

SEXUAL MORALITY

The attitude toward sexual morality in the Hellenistic world was, by Jewish or Christian standards, very flexible. Most of the writers of the period reflect considerable freedom in matters of sex, especially as far as men are concerned.

Premarital Sexual Morals

In almost every play by Terence and Plautus courtesans figure prominently in plot; brothels are common. The need for brothels to satisfy young men is defended by the elder Cato on the grounds that they are the lesser of two evils. "For when shameful Passion has swelled the veins," he writes, "tis well that you men come down hither, rather than tamper with other men's wives."[68] Cicero makes a similar plea in his defence of Caelius.

> For by common consent a young man is allowed some dalliance, and the nature herself is prodigal of youthful passions; and if they do find a vent so as not to shatter anyone's life, nor to ruin anyone's home they are generally regarded as easy to put up with.[69]

Even Alexander Severus, who was considered among the more noble of the emperors, provided his provincial governors with concubines if they were unmarried.[70] In a similar vein, Horace points out in detail the reasons for leaving married women alone in affairs of the heart.[71] Even the Stoic Epictetus advises: "In your sex life preserve purity, as far as you can, before marriage, and, if you do indulge, take only the privileges which are lawful."[72]

Premarital relations in Roman society were almost always heterosexual in nature. The Roman way, however, was influenced by the Greeks. There are, therefore, references to homosexual relations, such as Sallust's comment about those who gave themselves to unnatural vices;[73] but certainly the practice was neither as widespread or acceptable as in Greek culture.[74] The fact that the Romans had no god, either of their own religions or among those imported, to represent homosexuality suggests that it was never idealized as it was among the Greeks.

Postmarital Sexual Morals

From the earliest times in Rome, adultery constituted sufficient grounds for divorce. Adultery, however, was defined as the wife's infraction of the marital union.[75] There are numerous examples of extra-marital relations of both husbands and wives. Seutonius reports the profligacy of the Emperors Tiberius,[76] Caligula,[77] Domitian,[78] and Augustus.[79] According to Juvenal, Messalina, the wife of the Emperor Claudius, at times played the part of a harlot in a common brothel.[80] Many of these reports, however, should be dismissed as sensational fiction, Kiefer believes.[81] If it is a mistake to take all such reports seriously, it is equally a mistake to dismiss them all. It is certain that some of the emperors who legislated against adultery and prostitution were themselves the worst offenders. Thus Juvenal complains that the crows are absolved while the pigeons are judged.[82] The same sort of license existed among many of the aristocracy. References to adultery among this class are frequent. Juvenal[83] tells of Eppia, a senator's wife, who ran off with a gladiator; and Suetonius[84] speaks of a knight who was absolved of his oath not to divorce his wife when she was discovered in an adulterous relation with her son-in-law. Ovid was certainly not without an interested public for his work *The Art of Love* which dealt with: (a) where to find a mistress, (b) how to keep her, and (c) advice to the mistress on the means of pleasing her lover. Their attitude can be expressed in the words of the oration *Against Neaera*, falsely attributed to Demosthenes: "Mistresses we keep for the sake of pleasure, concubines for the daily care of our persons, but wives to bear us legitimate children . . ."[85]

The majority of the above literary references to immorality actually reflect only the conditions existing among the aristocracy. The question naturally arises whether or not this is a valid indication of morals in general. There are several factors which indicate that all classes of Roman society shared the same moral tone. For one thing, the common people were imitators of the patricians. Seneca, in speaking of the influence noble ladies had on others, laments that they thus pass on their shameful immorality to other women.[86] There is also some indication as to public morality in the plays of Plautus and in Petronius' *Satiricon*, which use the morals of the freedmen as material. And finally, there is ample evidence that the situation among the slaves, who were forbidden marriage, was notoriously immoral. It is Martial who speaks of the difficult task of attempting to discern the paternity of the various children in a troupe of slaves.[87]

Of special significance in evaluating the prevalence of immorality among the Romans is that it was made the subject matter for comedies. Comedy, perhaps more than any other dramatic form, must be in touch with life to be effective.[88] To a lesser degree, the same can be said about satire. The satirist writes expecting people to know what he is talking about. It is true that a satirist can exaggerate as a literary device, but no one accuses the Roman satirists of inventing.[89] It must, in all fairness, be realized that Juvenal, as well as Martial and Tacitus, paint the scenes of life only in somber hues; there were, of course, brighter colors on the palette, but they preferred the others because they saw life only on its dark side. There are many examples of fidelity and marital harmony in the literature of this period. Mallonia killed herself rather than submit to the advance of Tiberius,[90] and both Arria and Pauline committed suicide rather than live without their husbands.[91] Preisker[92] notes that the great value of Roman legislation in this respect is to elevate women and protect marriage.

An important factor in the moral view of Roman society was that "everything relating to sex was regarded as completely natural, and was approached far more simply and innocently than it is now."[93] For this reason, premarital relations were tolerated and there was no statutory punishment for adultery. Even the moral reforms of Augustus, while dealing with sexual license, had the declining birth rate and not ethics as its primary concern. This characteristic Roman apathy toward adultery is reflected in the situation related by Pliny of a military tribune's wife who was involved with a centurion; Pliny was more concerned about the husband's desire to take the wife back than he was with the fact of adultery.[94] Similarly, a knight was omitted from the list of jurors, according to Suetonius, because he had taken back a wife divorced for adultery.[95] Given such a lack of concern, it is not surprising that when Dio Cassius became consul there were 3,000 cases of adultery on the docket waiting trial.[96] If in later times adultery grew less common, it was not because of moral reform, but because "the facilities for divorce had, as it were, legitimized adultery by anticipation."[97] The moral situation was also complicated by the scarcity of women in the free class of society,[98] and the availability of slave-prostitutes.[99] Even religion in Rome did not contribute to moral control; the worship of Bacchus, Cybele, and Isis encouraged rather than discouraged promiscuous conduct. It should not be concluded, however, that this period was unique for moral degeneracy. Seneca warns:

> You are wrong, Lucilius, if you think that our age is peculiar for vice, luxury, desertion of moral standards, and all other things which everyone imputes to his own time. These are faults of mankind, not of

> any age. No time in history has been free from guilt.[100]

While Seneca was correct in asserting that his age was not the worst in regard to morals, it was still sufficiently bad for historians of morals to describe it as "loose in the extreme"[101] and as "extremely low."[102] The general indifference to sex morality in the Roman world is sharply set forth by Tacitus, who, when contrasting the morals of his own culture with those of the Germans, concludes: "No one laughs at vice there, no one calls seduction, suffered or wrought, the spirit of the age."[103]

CONCLUSIONS

From the earliest times, marriage in Roman society was monogamous, although there were various degrees of this relationship depending upon the degree to which the woman was under the man's domination. While marriage was viewed as the normal relationship, philosophical and religious tendencies arose to depreciate matrimony. This tendency grew to such proportions that it affected the birth rate in the Empire and became the subject of legislation. It found strong expression in a widespread prejudice against remarriage after the death of a mate.

Divorce was always a possibility among the Romans. While divorce was originally the prerogative of the husbands in marriages involving absolute authority, by the time of Christianity either party could obtain a divorce. This right to divorce was frequently employed, as indicated by the Augustian laws, to discourage divorce.

Premarital sexual relations, at least for men, were accepted as normal and inevitable and on this basis prostitution was accepted as a necessity. Extra-marital relations were almost always heterosexual in nature, the idealization of homosexual contacts in Greek culture being absent in the Roman world. Adultery and fornication were not uncommon in any class of society as sex did not come under legal or religious restrictions.

Chapter II Footnotes

[1]Adolf Harnack, *The Expansion of Christianity in the First Three Centuries,* trans. James Moffatt (New York: G. P. Putnam's Sons, 1905), II, 457-462.

[2]Edward Westermarck, *The History of Human Marriage* (London: The Macmillan Company, 1921), III, 49.

[3]Gaius, *Institutes,* i. 100.

[4]Rudolph Sohm, *The Institutes of Roman Law,* trans. James Ledlie (Oxford: Clarendon Press, 1892), p. 365.

[5]Dionysius, *Roman Antiquities,* ii. 25.

[6]*Ibid.*

[7]Tacitus, *Annals,* iv. 16.

[8]Percy Corbett, *The Roman Law of Marriage* (Oxford: Clarendon Press, 1930), p. 71.

[9]Gaius, *Institutes,* ii. 35.

[10]Corbett, *op. cit.*, p. 78.

[11]W. A. Becker, *Gallus; or Roman Scenes of the Time of Augustus,* trans. Frederick Metcalfe (London: John W. Parker, 1844), p. 174.

[12]Gaius, *Institutes,* i. 111.

[13]W. W. Fowler, *Social Life at Rome in the Age of Cicero* (New York: The Macmillan Company, 1909), p. 138.

[14]Jerome Carcopino, *Daily Life in Ancient Rome,* trans. E. O. Lorimer (New Haven: Yale University Press, 1941), p. 77.

[15]*Ibid.*, p. 138.

[16]*Epictetus,* III, xxii. 78, 82.

[17]*Epistle,* cxvi. 5. ff.

[18]J. S. Reid, "Asceticism (Roman)," *Encyclopaedia of Religion and Ethics,* ed. James Hastings (New York: Charles Scribner's Sons, 1928), II, p. 109.

[19]*Enneadas,* iii. 5.1.

[20]*Ibid.*, iv. 3.13.

[21]J. S. Reid, *op. cit.*, p. 109.

[22]Tibullus, i. 3.23.

[23]*Amores,* i. 8.73.

[24]*Valerius Maximus,* ii. i. 1.

[25]*Gellius,* i. 6.

[26] *Ibid.*, 1. 6.6.
[27] *Augustus*, xxxiv.
[28] *Cassius Dio*, liv. 16.
[29] *Digesta*, xlviii. 508.
[30] *Annals*, iii. 25.
[31] Sohm, *op. cit.*, p. 384.
[32] L. Friedlander, *Moeurs romaines du règne d'Auguste à la fin des Antonins*, trans. C. Vogel (Paris: C. Reinwald, 1865), I, 411.
[33] *Aeneid*, iv. 28.
[34] Otto Kiefer, *Sexual Life in Ancient Rome* (London: George Routledge and Sons, 1934), p. 39.
[35] *Diodorus Siculus*, xii. 12.
[36] Capitolius, *Marcus Aurelius*, iii. 4.
[37] *Germania*, xix.
[38] *Silvae*, ii. 3.
[39] *Dionysius*, ii. 25.
[40] *Institutes*, i. 137.
[41] *Dionysius*, ii. 25.
[42] Plutarch, *Romulus*, xxii.
[43] *Ibid.*
[44] *Valerius Maximus*, ii. 9. 2.
[45] *Ibid.*, v. 3.10-12.
[46] *Ibid.*
[47] Plutarch, *Amilius Paulus*, v. 6.
[48] Plutarch, *Cicero*, xli. 7.
[49] *To His Friends*, viii. 7.
[50] Kiefer, *op. cit.*, p. 31.
[51] Plutarch, *Pompey*, iv. 10.
[52] Plutarch, *Cicero*, xli. 187-189.
[53] Pliny, *Natural History*, vii. 158.
[54] Plutarch, *Cato Minor*, xxxvi. 52.
[55] Carcopino, *op. cit.*, p. 97.
[56] *Epigrams*, vi. 7.
[57] *Satire*, vi. 224-230.
[58] *On Benefits*, iii. 16. 2.
[59] *Ibid.*
[60] Becker, *op. cit.*, p. 117.

[61]Sohm, *op. cit.*, p. 382.
[62]*Satire*, vi. 142-155.
[63]Sohm, *op. cit.*, p. 372.
[64]*Ulpian*, vi. 12-13.
[65]Sohm, *op. cit.*, p. 384.
[66]*Epigrams*, vi. 4.
[67]Cassius, *Dio's Roman History*, lxxvi, 16.4.
[68]Horace, *Satires*, i. 2. 23-26.
[69]Cicero, *Pro Caelio*, xii, 28.
[70]Lampridius, *Severus Alexander*, xlii, 4.
[71]Horace, *Satires*, i. 2.
[72]Epictetus, *Encheiridion*, viii.
[73]Sallust, *Bellum Catilinae*, xii.
[74]Hans Licht (pseud. Paul Brandt), *Sexual Life in Ancient Greece* (New York: Barnes and Noble, 1952), p. 436.
[75]W. E. H. Lecky, *History of European Morals from Augustus to Charlemagne* (New York: George Brazimiller, 1955), p. 312.
[76]Suetonius, *Tiberius*, xliii-xlvi.
[77]Suetonius, *Caligula*, xxiv-xxv.
[78]Suetonius, *Domitian*, i. 3.
[79]Suetonius, *Augustus*, lxxi.
[80]Juvenal, *Satires*, vi. 114.
[81]Otto Kiefer, *op. cit.*, p. 62.
[82]Juvenal, *Satires*, ii. 63.
[83]Juvenal, *Satires*, vi. 103.
[84]Suetonius, *Tiberius*, xxxv.
[85]*Against Neaera*, cxxii.
[86]Seneca, *On Benefits*, iii. 16.1.
[87]Martial, *Epigrams*, vi. 39.
[88]Edith Hamilton, *The Roman Way to Western Civilization* (New York: The New American Library, 1957), p. 10.
[89]Samuel Dill, *Roman Society from Nero to Marcus Aurelius* (London: Macmillan Company, 1920), p. 87.
[90]Suetonius, *Tiberius*, xiv.
[91]Pliny, *Epistles*, iii. 16; Tacitus, *Annals*, xv. 63-64.
[92]Herbert Preisker, *Christentum und Ehe in den ersten drei Jahrhunderten* (Berlin: Trowitzsch, 1927), p. 66.
[93]Otto Kiefer, *op. cit.*, p. 57.

[94]Pliny, *Letters,* vi. 31.
[95]Suetonius, *Domitian,* viii. 3.
[96]Dio Cassius, *Roman History,* lxxvii. 4.
[97]Carcopino, *op. cit.*, p. 95.
[98]Dio Cassius, *Roman History,* l. 16.
[99]Martial, *Epigrams,* vi. 66.
[100]Seneca, *Epistle,* xcvii.
[101]W. W. Fowler, *op. cit.*, p. 157.
[102]W. E. H. Lecky, *op. cit.*, p. 308.
[103]Tacitus, *Germania,* xix.

CHAPTER III

THE BACKGROUND OF JEWISH MARRIAGE

The Christian religion grew out of a Jewish soil. Judaism supplied both the first disciples and the moral tone for the new movement. It is appropriate in an appraisal of the Christian doctrine of marriage and divorce, therefore, to survey the Jewish position. Fortunately, there are many references to the institution of marriage in Jewish literature. The literary corpus includes the Old Testament, the Mishnah, and the Talmud. Especially pertinent are the tractates: *Kiddushin* (on betrothment); *Kethuboth* (on marriage deeds); *Yebamoth* (on levirate and prohibited marriages); *Sotah* (on the suspected adulteress); and *Gittin* (on divorce). Occasional references are found in the Apocrypha, the Pseudepigrapha, and in the writings of Josephus and Philo.

MARRIAGE

The institution of marriage has been held in highest regard in Judaism. The literature abounds with passages which extol the blessings of matrimony.

Object of Praise

The creation stories in the Old Testament provide a religious rationale for marital union. From the beginning the first couple received God's blessing.[1] The sanctity of marriage is reflected in the injunction against adultery and the imposition of the death penalty for breach of it.[2] The Wisdom Literature is especially eloquent in its praise for matrimony. The man who marries has a "good thing" in a wife and thereby obtains "favor with the Lord."[3] A "good woman" is considered a "crown" to her husband.[4] Her value is lauded in the poem which begins: "A good wife who can find? She is far more precious than jewels."[5] The attitude of the writers of the Wisdom Literature is summed up by Gasper who says, "For the Wisdom writers, as for all Orientals, life without a home, wife, and family is unthinkable—a sorry makeshift at best."[6] The same tone is continued in the Apocrypha. Tobit quotes the creation story in regard to his union with Sara, denying that it is merely to satisfy lusts.[7] Sara had prayed to the Lord for a marriage partner.[8] In the Book of Susanna, the heroine prefers death rather than to violate her marriage through adultery with the two elders.[9]

Rabbinical writings of the Tannaitic period are equally profuse in their commendation of marriage. The purpose of marriage was to fulfill the will of God.[10] Other motives, such as gaining wealth, were depreciated.[11] Indeed, the man who has a noble wife is in reality already rich.[12]

Indicative of the rabbis' evaluation are the concessions they made to the married. It was permissible to sell a scroll of the Law, if the money was needed for marriage.[13] When a man married, his sins were forgiven him.[14] Study of the law should be postponed until after marriage. To be single was to be "without joy, without blessing, without religion, without protection, without peace."[15] The man who took a wife, however, was perfect.[16] When a woman asked Judah B. Simon what God had been doing since creation, the rabbi's reply was that he had been busy arranging marriages, although he admitted that sometimes God found this more difficult than dividing the Red Sea.[17] God dwells with the faithful husband and bride.[18] The husband is not left without instructions as to how he should treat his wife. As long as he loves her like himself and honors her more, he will have peace.[19] If he afflicts her, God will count her tears.[20] If a marriage is dissolved God hates the one who puts away his wife and tears are shed on God's altar on her behalf.[21] The world is darkened for a widower.[22] Watching a wife die is like being present at the destruction of the Temple.[23]

Worthy of special mention in a survey of the Jewish attitude toward matrimony, is the prophetic employment of marriage as a figure to represent the relationship between Yahweh and Israel. Hosea speaks of the covenant in the vocabulary of a betrothal.[24] Isaiah refers to Yahweh as the "husband" of Israel.[25] Jeremiah pictures their relationship as a "bride's love."[26] These, and other expressions, could be possible only if marriage was held in the highest regard.

Forms of Marriage

Nowhere in the Old Testament is the form of marriage regulated by divine decree. The literature of the Jews reflects both polygamy and monogamy.

Polygamy.—Polygamy is evident in numerous examples of family life in the Old Testament. Among the heroes, Abraham, Jacob, and David had a plurality of wives. The common sociological explanations for polygamy are rejected by Mace,[27] who agrees with many biblical scholars that such unions were motivated by the desire for progeny.[28]

Although plural marriages were legal, it is doubtful if they were ever frequent among the common people. The economic problem of maintaining an additional wife would be prohibitive for many.[29] Exposing the home to strife would also mitigate plural marriages. It is interesting to note that the word "rival" became the technical term for the second wife in such unions.[30] This type of hostility is manifested in the cases of Sarah and Hagar, and Leah and Rachel. Certain biblical laws were equally discouraging to polygamy. Sisters could not marry the same man.[31] The interests of the less favored wife were zealously guarded.[32] In the Talmud the first wife was permitted a divorce if her husband took another wife without her consent.[33]

Among the forms of the polygamous union practiced by the Jews was concubinage. Women who were involved in such unions were either Jewish girls who, because of poverty, had been sold into slavery[34] or foreign women taken in war or purchased.[35] When children were born, the concubine's status was raised and safeguarded by law.[36] Before the beginning of the Common Era, concubinage had disappeared.[37]

Regardless of the infrequency, plural marriages were legal and undoubtedly occurred. Justin Martyr chides Trypho for the practice.[38] Even the Romans, long champions of monogamy, had to make an allowance for the custom of the Jews.[39] Polygamy especially lent itself to temporary marriages in different locales.[40] Apparently the first self-imposed legal restriction was made at the Rabbinical Synod at Worms at the beginning of the eleventh century of the Common Era.[41]

Monogamy.—The tendency in most societies for marriage to evolve into monogamous relations was also operative in Judaism.[42] Certain of her heroes, judging from information available in Scripture, lived in such unions; Adam, Noah, Isaac, Joseph, and Job were among that number. Monogamy is presented as the original form of marriage.[43] It is among the descendants of Cain that the first plural marriage occurs.[44] The frequent occurrence of the figure of the Yahweh-Israel marriage in the prophets reflects a monogamous idea. Probably by the time of the prophets monogamy was the prevalent form.[45] Any defection from the worship of God on the part of the people was termed "adultery" in the prophet's vocabulary.[46] All the scenes of domestic happiness in the Wisdom Literature assume monogamy.[47] Similar exaltations of single unions appear in the Mishnah.[48] There is nothing in the references to matrimony in the papyri of Elephantine to suggest any form other than monogamy.[49] The Zadokite Document makes explicit its views on the subject of marriage.[50] The prohibition it makes against plural marriages, Rowley states, was "stricter . . . than was common among other Jewish groups of their time."[51] The inscriptions pertaining to the Jews of the Diaspora indicate monogamy.[52] It is true, however, that the Greek word ἀντίζηλης occurs twice in the book of Ecclesiasticus (26:8-9; 37:11) and can be taken as references to polygamy. The fact that Ben Sira, always outspoken against common evils, is silent on this point is taken by Charles[53] as an additional indication of the decline of polygamy. In fact, there is unanimity among scholars that polygamy was on the wane among the Jews before the beginning of the Common Era.[54]

Androgynous Man

Important in the rabbinical idea of marriage, and in itself an argument for monogamy, is the doctrine of the androgynous man. The basis for it is found in Genesis 1:27 which reads, "So God created man in his own image, in the image of God he created him; male and female created he them." The important thing to notice is the shift from the singular "man" and "him" in the first part of the passage to "male and female" and "them" in the latter portion of the verse. Upon this change it has been concluded that Adam was a composite being; that is, man and woman together make a unit of one. This concept was not unique with the rabbis; it is found in Plato's *Symposium* in the mouth of Aristophanes.

> First, then, human beings were formerly not divided into two sexes, male and female; ... The androgynous sex, both in appearance and in name, was common both to male and female; it's name alone remains, which labours under a reproach.[55]

This is suggested by Daube[56] to be the source of the idea in rabbinic thought. Grunwald[57] believes the concept of androgynous man was adopted by the rabbis in order to reconcile the apparently conflicting statements of the Bible. Whatever its origin and purpose, the concept occurs several times in rabbinical writings.

> R. Jeremiah b. Leazar said: When the Holy One, blessed be He, created Adam, He created him as hermaphrodite, for it is said, male and female created He them and called their name Adam.[58]
>
> A single man is not a whole man. God called their name man.[59]
>
> R. Hiyya b. Gomdi said: He is also incomplete, for it is written, And he blessed them, and called their name Adam, i.e., man.[60]

The same idea is expressed in the Zadokite Document where it is used, along with the fact that the animals went into the ark two by two, as an argument for monogamy.[61] It is also alluded to by Philo in his work *On the Creation*.[62] The myth that man and woman together form man has been used as an argument against both polygamy and divorce.

Depreciation of Marriage

Judaism begins with the basic assumption that since man is the creation of God, no element of his nature can be inherently evil. Marriage is regarded not as a concession to the weakness of the human flesh, but as a sacred duty. It is unusual, therefore, for matrimony to be disparaged in the biblical and Jewish traditions.

Abstinence.—The spirit of asceticism was largely missing from Judaism, especially sexual abstinence. Even the Nazarite, who came closest to the ascetic figure, was not required to forego marriage.[63] The Nazarite prohibitions, the dietary observations, and other similar practices were not actually ascetic in origin since they did not spring from a desire to suppress natural instincts and life.[64] That the Law was adverse to sexual abstinence is seen in legislation against mutilation.[65] In all of the Old Testament there is no example of celibacy being freely embraced. While it is true there was a temporary continence imposed on the priests who officiated in the Temple, it was a matter of ceremonial uncleanliness to be avoided by the sacerdotal class. Celibacy was also undoubtedly imposed on some because of poverty, but it was not the ideal.[66] Where celibacy did occur in Judaism, for example, among the Therapeutae and Essenes as mentioned by Josephus,[67] it was only among the peripheral groups. Kohler[68] finds the rationale for such abstinence in the desire for a revelation, just as the people refrained from intercourse when God revealed himself to Moses. Not all the sects practiced celibacy, however, as the Qumran Community indicates.[69] The only other support of sexual abstinence occurs under the influence of non-Jewish philosophy. Thus, the author of the Wisdom of Solomon can praise the "barren" and the "eunuch."[70] Such [illegible]cism, Moore[71] maintains, left no impact upon o[illegible] Judaism. As Cole[72] observes, in a society where "love" and its cognates are used in religious writings for both the love of God and sensual love, and where the Song of Solomon, a hymn in praise of sexual love, received a place in the sacred canon, there could not be any thorough-going depreciation of sex.

The rabbis employed strong invectives against those men who did not marry. The bachelor was one who had shed blood, some taught.[73] Others said he was guilty of impairing the divine likeness.[74] In spurning matrimony, the bachelor not only failed to fulfill the law of procreation, but he also made himself susceptible to temptation. A woman was not regarded by the rabbis to be under the obligation of procreation.[75] She could, therefore, choose to marry or remain single.

Digamy.—The lack of sympathy in Judaism for the ascetic life is indicated by the absence of any prejudice against digamy, that is, the remarriage of a widow or widower. A *levir* was required by the law to marry his brother's childless widow.[76] The purpose in taking the deceased husband's brother was to raise up a son for the dead man.[77] In situations other than the *levirate,* there is nothing to indicate that a second marriage after the death of a mate was unusual. Judith declined a second marriage in order to serve God, but her husband's wealth enabled her to make this decision which would be denied to others.[78] Certainly rabbinical literature presupposes the right to remarry after the death of a partner. Witnesses to the death or an identification of the body were required, but these were safeguards against a premature marriage and were not intended to discourage digamy.[79] Perhaps the clearest indication of the acceptance of second marriages was the regulation that a priest should be prohibited from marrying a divorced woman; he could, however, marry a widow.[80]

DIVORCE

That divorce was practiced by the Jews of biblical times is evident in passages which presuppose the institution. Special legislation prevented the priest from marrying a woman who had been "put away" by her husband.[81] A priest's daughter who was divorced was permitted to return to her father's home.[82] The vows of a divorced woman were still obligatory, although she might subsequently remarry.[83] A man was denied the right to divorce his wife if he had either charged her falsely with premarital unchastity, or if before their marriage they had been discovered in *flagrante delicto*.[84] The principal relevant passage in the Old Testament, however, is found in the twenty-fourth chapter of Deuteronomy.

> When a man takes a wife and marries her, if then she finds no favor in his eyes because he has found some indecency in her, and he writes her a bill of divorce and puts it in her hand and sends her out of his house, and she departs out of his house, and if she goes and becomes another man's wife, and the latter husband dislikes her and writes her a bill of divorce and puts it in her hand and sends her out of his house, or if the latter husband dies, who took her to be his wife, then her former husband, who sent her away, may not take her again to be his wife after she has been defiled; for that is an abominable act before the Lord, and you shall not bring guilt upon the land which the Lord God gives you for an inheritance.[85]

This passage obviously contains a conditional sentence. Both the King James Version and the American Standard Version make the apodosis occur in the first verse. While these two translations are slightly different in their arrangement of the apodosis, the force of both is to emphasize that a divorce is to be obtained if some uncleanness is found in the wife. It is possible, however, to construct the conditional sentence in a different manner. The Revised Standard Version, quoted above, makes the apodosis occur in the fourth verse. The Septuagint, as well as later commentators,[86] agrees with this rendering. The significance of this construction is that it does not make divorce mandatory although it shows that divorce was practiced and apparently sanctioned. The force of the passage is that a man, having divorced his wife, cannot take her back if she has subsequently remarried and been divorced.

Grounds for Divorce

This passage in Deuteronomy indicates that divorce was to be based on definite grounds called "uncleanness." The word "uncleanness" (*'erwat dabar*) means the "nakedness or shame of a thing." There is, however, no unanimity among scholars as to what constitutes uncleanness. In the Old Testament the word occurs, in addition to the above-mentioned passage, only in Deuteronomy 23:14. There it is translated "anything indecent" by the Revised Standard Version in a context that obviously refers to uncovered excrement and not to sexual conduct. In both places the Septuagint employs ἀσχήμων which has the same ambiguity.

Opinion about the meaning of "uncleanness" was sharply divided among the rabbis. This was, in fact, one of the points on which the famous schools of Shammai and Hillel differed. Shammai, who was often characterized by a strict and rigorous interpretation of the Law, limited the meaning of the word to sexual immorality.

The School of Shammai says: A man may not

> divorce his wife unless he has found unchastity in her, for it is written, because he hath found in her indecency in anything.[87]

A more lenient position was taken by Hillel's School.

> And the School of Hillel says: [He may divorce her] even if she spoiled a dish for him, for it is written, Because he hath found in her indecency in anything.[88]

A later disciple of Hillel included as sufficient reason for divorce the finding of a more pleasing woman.[89] Although there is no biblical example of a man lightly putting away his wife, Hillel's interpretation is more in keeping with the meaning of the Hebrew words. Mielziner[90] suggests that Hillel took this position to prevent the greater wrong of frequent adultery in a time of moral corruption. Whatever the motives may have been, the lenient position became normative for Judaism.[91] This is reflected by Josephus.

> He that desires to be divorced from his wife for any cause whatsoever (and many such causes happen among men), let him in writing give assurance that he will never use her as his wife any more; for by this means she may be at liberty to marry another husband . . .[92]

This lenient position is also supported by Philo who speaks of the possibility of a woman being divorced by her husband "under any pretense whatever."[93] Even the two circumstances where biblical law prohibited a man from divorcing his wife (that is, in the case of the seducer and in the case of a husband who falsely accuses his wife of ante-nuptial incontinence) were modified by the oral law to permit divorce.[94]

While Jewish men may have had considerable latitude in obtaining divorces, there is nothing to indicate that divorce was frequently used. The preacher in Malachi laments the practice of divorce.[95] There are many rabbinical passages which discourage the custom. Apparently, it was a rare thing among the rabbis themselves. The most prominent case was that of Rabbi Jose who divorced his wife. When she and her new husband fell on hard times, he took them in.[96]

Barrenness.—Probably the most common cause for divorce was that of the wife's barrenness.[97] The husband had a God-given obligation to produce children. If part of God's law was to marry and be fruitful, then it was not only lawful and expedient for the husband of a barren woman to take another wife, but it was also a duty.[98] More merit was attached to procreation than was associated with the building of the Temple.[99] In the event the couple was childless, it was customary to wait ten years before barrenness was assumed.[100]

Adultery.— Certainly another frequent reason for divorce was adultery. According to the Jewish view of marriage, adultery could only be committed by the wife. The husband was permitted extra-marital relations since, in a polygamous system, every woman was a prospective wife, unless she was married. That is, a husband could not violate his own marriage.[101] The majority of the sex offenses among the Jews could probably fall into the category of adultery since most of the women, except the very young, would either be betrothed or married.

Adultery was viewed as a serious sin. The Decalogue cites it as a sin against God.[102] Adultery thus becomes a concern of the community since it affects the people's relationship with God.[103] Involved in the act of adultery is a disobedience to God's law; a trespass against the husband; a condemnation of the children born to such unions to bastardy; and defilement of one's own name.[104] Whatever other virtues one might have, according to the rabbis, they could not save the adulterer from Gehenna.[105] Adultery, idolatry, and murder, were the sins which the rabbis prohibited the Jews from committing even though refusal during the days of Hadrian might cost the Jew his life.[106]

The act of adultery was considered irremediable. The death penalty was required by the Law for the adulteress and her partner.[107] The sentence was only carried out when the two were taken in *flagrante delicto*. Since two eye witnesses were required, it is unlikely that executions were common. Such punishment was rare in the Tannaitic age.[108] Abrahams[109] can find only one example of the death penalty in the Mishnah, and it does not fall within the lifetime of Jesus. Although Josephus[110] mentions the sentence, in context it appears to be an antiquarian note. The Romans had deprived the Jewish courts of the right of capital punishment.[111] The *Pericope de Adultera* of the Gospel of John[112] is only a theoretical discussion since only the woman is brought to Jesus, even though the couple had been apprehended in the act. In those cases where there was only the suspicion of adultery, the woman was given the ordeal of bitter waters.[113] An appropriate ceremony was accompanied by drinking in solution dust swept from the Temple floor. If she were guilty, certain physical calamities would befall her. This rite apparently remained in vogue until the moral breakdown which accompanied the Jewish wars with Rome.[114] After the abolition of the death penalty, a husband was required to divorce his adulterous wife, even if he were willing to condone her conduct.[115] If the adultery was only suspected, then a divorce was optional with the husband.

Who Could Divorce

The right of divorce belonged only to the husband. Divorce was basically a driving out of the house. Since the husband owned the property, this would have been impossible for the wife to accomplish.[116] The bill of divorcement, which was to make one free to marry another, was likewise inappropriate for the man for he always had the right in a polygamous society to marry another. The right of divorce was also impossible for the wife since she had no forum in which to obtain redress.[117] Josephus[118] does mention two women who divorced their husbands, but both were Hellenists at heart and were following the Gentile practice. In referring to Salome, Herod's sister,

Josephus specifically states that her action "was not according to Jewish laws."[119]

The inability of the wife to institute divorce proceedings does not mean she was entirely without recourse. In certain cases she could compel her husband to divorce her, but even then it was considered still to be the husband who was exercising his prerogative. How essentially divorce was the right of the husband is seen in the circumstances where the wife had been deserted. In such cases there could be no divorce because there was no man to instigate the procedure.[120] The biblical background for a wife compelling her husband to divorce her was found by the rabbis in Exodus[121] where it is stated that a bondwoman who has been elevated to the position of a wife, if mistreated, has the right to go free. If such a right belonged to the bondwoman, reasoned the rabbis, it must belong to the free woman.[122] The grounds upon which the wife could sue for divorce were carefully regulated by the rabbis. If the wife had sufficient reason for divorce, and the husband refused, he was subject to the thirty-nine stripes.[123]

Conjugal Rights.— Conjugal rights were subject to regulation by the Law. Taking another wife did not diminish this right of the first wife.[124] The length of time a man could abstain from intercourse, depending on his occupation, was limited before he was subject to a monetary fine. Any prolonged abstinence meant the husband was required to put her away.[125]

Sterility.—The sterility of the husband was valid

ground for the wife to seek a dissolution of the union.[126] According to the Talmud, such a marriage could only be considered childless after ten years. If there was some doubt as to which mate was afflicted, the presumption was that the husband was sterile.[127]

Liberty.—The husband has the right, according to the book of Numbers,[128] to annul any vows his wife might make. If by taking a vow, she has deprived herself of any privilege, and the husband refuses to annul that vow, the wife is entitled to a divorce.[129] This was interpreted to be the same as if the husband had taken a vow which placed restrictions upon his wife. Among the restrictions of liberty which are serious enough to warrant divorce, the Mishnah names eating certain fruit, wearing certain apparel or adornment, going to her father's house, and visiting either a house of mourning or a house of feasting.[130]

Blemishes.—If the husband suffered some unpleasant disease or was engaged in some malodorous business which rendered cohabitation difficult, then the wife could obtain a divorce.[131] This was possible provided she had not specifically waived the right to divorce before the marriage.[132] Among the circumstances which provided sufficient grounds for divorce were an affliction of boils or polypus and the occupations of the coppersmith and tanner.[133]

Support.—A husband was under obligation to provide the necessities of life for his bride; what constituted the minimum was regulated in the Mishnah.[134] In the event the husband failed to provide the essentials, the wife could request a divorce.[135]

Charge of Incontinence.—If the husband, seeking to be free of his wife, makes a false charge of ante-nuptial incontinence, the wife is entitled to a divorce.[136] Philo felt that an appropriate punishment for such culprits would be to make them remain married to the woman they have sought to put away.[137]

Possible Desertion.—Although a wife could not receive a divorce if her husband deserted her, she could safeguard her position. If her husband desired to move to another country and she feared he was going to abandon her, she could require him to give her a bill of divorcement before he departed.[138] There is nothing to indicate that desertions were common. It was not a grave problem, Paterson contends,[139] until the period of the Talmud and the social upheavals which accompanied the military invasions of Palestine.

Apostasy.—An Israelite who had apostatized from his faith was still bound to his Jewish bride.[140] If she so desired, the wife could secure a divorce. Since her husband was no longer a Jew under Jewish authority, it was permissible to appeal to a Gentile court to carry out the action.[141]

Restraint of Divorce

While the right of divorce was not modified by the rabbis, the entire course of law and custom was to increase the practical difficulties in obtaining one. Numerous passages in the Talmud lament the abuse of the right.

> Over him who divorces the wife of his youth, even the altar of God sheds tears.[142]

> He who marries her that is divorced from her husband because of her evil conduct, is worthy of death; for he has taken a wicked woman into his house.[143]

> He that putteth her (his wife) away is hated of God.[144]

The tendency to discourage divorce found three avenues of expression. First, there was an elaboration and expansion of the requirements for the bill of divorcement. Second, there was the requirement that the wife's dowry be repaid in the event of divorce. Third, there was a multiplication of the circumstances in which a divorce was impossible.

Bill of Divorcement.—The bill of divorcement was a part of the legislation in the book of Deuteronomy.[145] It is specifically stated that the husband is to write her a bill and put it in her hand. A similar bill is mentioned in the book of Isaiah.[146] In both passages the impression is given that the bill is a long-established tradition. Gordon[147] has indicated from other Semitic cultures that the words, "Because she is not my wife and I am not her husband," in Hosea 2:4-5 are in reality the formula for divorce. Even if his conclusion is not accepted, the bill in biblical times must have been simple in nature. According to the *Mishnah*, the essential part of the document was the formula, "Lo, thou art free to marry any man."[148] The only biblical requirement was concerned with its delivery, that it be placed in the woman's hand. Both the document and its delivery became the subject of rabbinical control.

The document must be written by one person and witnessed by others.[149] It had to be composed for the particular occasion; blank forms were not acceptable.[150] Even the type of paper and ink were regulated.[151] The bill could not be thrown to or left for the wife, but must be placed either in her hand or within her reach.[152] Before a properly delivered and written bill is valid, the wife must comprehend its meaning.[153] In the event the document is lost while being delivered, the finder is not to return it.[154] Even minute restrictions are placed upon the person who makes the delivery.[155] Although many of the regulations concerning the bill are late in their development, they clearly show that the tendency among the rabbis was to impede divorce and to protect the rights of the wife.

Dowry.—Undoubtedly a successful check on divorce was the law which required the husband to repay the wife's dowry (*ketubah*) if the marriage was terminated. Such was the case with Rabbi Jose the Galilean who had a bad wife. He could not afford to divorce her until a group of his students made up a purse to pay back the dowry.[156]

Some of the rabbis considered the dowry to be Mosaic in origin,[157] although it was probably introduced during the last century of the First Commonwealth.[158] A similar practice, however, can be traced in the sections of the Old Testament which refer to Dinah,[159] Rebecca,[160] and the law of seduction.[161] Originally, the dowry was paid to the father of the bride, but eventually it came to be given to the wife and was undivided in the estate of her husband. [162] In this way it acted as a lien on his property. In most cases of divorce the dowry was returned to the wife, although she could forfeit it through misconduct. Among actions serious enough to cost the wife her dowry were certain transgressions of the Law and Jewish customs. The rabbis stated that:

> These are they that are put away without their *ketubah*: . . . if she gives her husband untithed food, or has a connection with him in her uncleanness, or does not set apart Dough-offering, or utters a vow and does not fulfill it.[163]

Serious breeches of Jewish customs were carefully defined:

> If she goes out with her hair unbound, or spins in the street, or speaks with any man. Abba Saul says: Also if she curses his parents in his presence. R. Tarfon says: Also [if she is] a scolding woman. And who is deemed a scolding woman? Whosoever speaks inside her house so that the neighbors hear her voice.[164]

Impossibility of Divorce.—The Old Testament lists two

situations in which divorce is impossible. One is if the wife has been falsely charged with premarital incontinence.[165] The other is in the case of a wife who had been seduced before marriage.[166] To these two, others are added in the *Mishnah.* Some rabbis maintained that a wife who was insane could not be divorced.[167] Neither could a wife who had been taken captive be divorced; the husband's duty under such circumstances was to ransom her back.[168]

Remarriage

The Old Testament assumes in the Deuteronomic passage the right of the divorced parties to remarry. Rabbinical law also assumes that remarriage would be the normal course. Thus the essential phrase of the bill of divorcement was, "Thou art free to any man." There were, however, certain restrictions placed on the right to remarry. Many of the rabbinical regulations pertain to the remarriage of the original couple. Such a reunion was impossible if the wife had subsequently married another man and divorced him before returning to her first husband.[169] This prohibition was binding even if she had been widowed by the second husband. In the event she remarried her first husband without regard to the prohibition, it was urged by Philo that the death penalty be enforced for adultery.[170] When capital punishment was impossible, there seems to have been an enforced separation.[171] If the woman had merely lived with another man without the benefit of marriage, then some rabbis felt it was permissible for her to remarry her husband.[172] A husband was prevented from remarrying his wife if he had put her away for suspicion of adultery,[173] or for barrenness,[174] or because of vows she had taken.[175]

Remarriage was prohibited in certain circumstances to guard against possible fraud. Reunion was impossible if a third party had supplied the dowry payment.[176] This apparently was to prevent the husband and wife from remarrying and thereby swindling the one who had put up the dowry. A husband who had consecrated all his property to religious purposes could not remarry.[177] This could have been a convenient means to free the amount of the dowry from the vow, had they been permitted to remarry.

Some general restrictions were placed on the right to marry a second time. Most of these were designed to prevent collusion in the matter of the divorce. A woman could not marry her suspected partner in adultery.[178] The man who delivered the bill of divorce was ineligible, as was a witness to her husband's death.[179] A divorced woman could not marry a priest.[180] A priest's life, Philo explains, must be free from the strife which might exist if his wife had a former husband.[181] In addition, there were some temporary impediments which were to guard the paternity or welfare of children. There was a mandatory waiting period of three months before another marriage could be arranged.[182] If the woman was pregnant or with a nursing child, the new marriage was postponed for an appropriate time.[183]

SEX MORALITY

Although Judaism permitted divorce, it did not condone extra-marital sex relations.[184] All of the Old Testament passages heretofore mentioned are definite on this matter. Josephus[185] insisted that the law recognized no other sexual connection than that of husband and wife. The rabbis, cognizant as they were of the evil intent of man, went to great lengths to safeguard purity. They constructed elaborate fences about the biblical law governing sex relations. Stress was placed on the importance of purity of mind. They could say, "The thought of sin is worse than sin itself."[186] Equal concern was given to the prevention of temptation. It was improper for a man to walk behind a woman,[187] to converse with a woman on the street,[188] and to gaze lustfully at a woman.[189] To listen to a woman sing or to see her hair was likewise prohibited.[190] A special source of temptation would be female slaves; accordingly, the rabbis warned that "the more bondwomen, the more lewdness." [191] Even with the combined effort of the rabbis, it would be expected that some would fall below the moral ideal.

Premarital Sexual Morals

With marriages normally arranged and consummated at an early age, opportunities for premarital relations would be limited. Frequently, girls were engaged while barely more than infants.[192] A common age for the marriage itself was twelve for the bride and eighteen for the groom.[193] Boys who reached the age of twenty-one unmarried were considered to be under a curse.[194] Such early unions helped to guard the people from temptation. This, of course, was not always successful. Sirach tells of all the difficulties a father has in watching over his daughters.[195] The delay of the Messiah's coming is blamed on the men who are frivolous with young girls.[196] In the event a man and an unmarried girl were discovered in a delicate situation, marriage was required.[197] Apparently a similar concern for virginity was not prevalent at Nuzi; there even a prostitute was viewed as equally desirable for marriage as a maiden.[198]

Prostitution, of course, was not unknown in Israel. It is reflected in the Old Testament stories of Tamar,[199] Rahab,[200] and Samson's relation with the harlot of Gaza.[201] In the earlier times, there existed both religious and secular prostitution. Eventually the former disappeared and a new situation arose after the Exile with the city harlot. She had special quarters in the city.[202] In her trade, she employed smooth words and seductive glances. The Wisdom Literature characterizes her in detail.[203] The "strange woman" in the Wisdom Literature has been variously identified as a Greek courtesan, a foreign or an Israelite prostitute. Humbert[204] has shown convincingly that she is not a prostitute, but a Jewish adulteress. Philo states that the Jews put to death harlots,[205] but there is no support of this from other sources. Although much is written to discourage the patrons of prostitution, the crime seems to be more that of folly than immorality.[206]

Postmarital Sexual Morals

The Jewish attitude toward polygamy placed the husband in a position of considerable latitude as far as postnuptial sex relations are concerned. Technically, he was allowed contacts outside of marriage since every woman was a potential wife. The husband could only commit adultery if his partner was a married woman. Polygamy, with its opportunities for sexual relations, was on the decline before the beginning of the Common Era. Not very many men could afford a plurality of wives. Equally important, the availability of eligible women would be a limiting factor. Even though prohibited, unions with Gentiles were frequent[207] and there seem to have been as many Jewesses involved in these mixed marriages as Jewish men.[208] Slavery and concubinage, major sources of women for extra-marital relations, were also on the wane before the Common Era.

There is obviously no way of ascertaining the statistics pertaining to sex morality. Certainly there were periods of moral lapses. The rite of bitter waters was eventually abandoned because during a national crisis adultery became too commonplace.[209] Also, a Babylonian *amora* complained that the Messiah was delaying his appearance because of prevalent fornication in his city.[210] But on the whole, the Jews enjoyed a good reputation for morality. Pride is taken in the virginity of Jewish girls both by Philo[211] and the rabbis.[212] So much higher was the morality of the Jews, when compared to their Gentile neighbors, that some rabbis considered as statutory non-virgins all Gentiles, captives, and slaves over three years old.[213] The Jewish propaganda of pseudo-Phocylides was written in part to encourage a higher morality among non-Jews. Although it is impossible completely to eliminate unchastity in a society, Jewish law worked toward that end through the prohibition of things evil in themselves, through attempts to control passions, and through the removal of opportunities for sin.[214] However gross individual conduct was, the two great shapers of morals, religion and customs, were united on the side of continence.

CONCLUSIONS

Marriage was held in the highest esteem in Judaism. This regard for matrimony was expressed in a disparagement of the single life and an absence of sexual asceticism. Remarriage after the death of a mate was a normal custom. Polygamy was legal, although not universally practiced. There are indications that plural marriages were on the wane before the beginning of the Common Era.

A divorce could be obtained upon trivial grounds. The tendency of rabbinical legislation was to discourage frequent divorce by regulating the institution. Technically the divorce was the prerogative of the husband, although under certain circumstances the wife could force her husband to divorce her. When the right of capital punishment was taken from the Jews, it became mandatory for a man to put away an adulterous wife. Divorced individuals were free to marry.

The moral tone of Judaism was very high. Rabbinical legislation was designed to prevent immoral situations from arising. Although many individuals undoubtedly fell below the Jewish standards, the Jews enjoyed a reputation for morality in the ancient world.

Chapter III Footnotes

[1]Gen. 1:28.
[2]Gen. 38:24.
[3]Prov. 18:22.
[4]Prov. 12:4.
[5]Prov. 31:10.
[6]J. W. Gasper, *Social Ideas in the Wisdom Literature* (Washington, D.C.: The Catholic University of America Press, 1947), p. 1.
[7]Tob. 8:6-7.
[8]Tob. 3:15.
[9]Susanna 1:23.
[10]Sotah 12a.
[11]Kid. 70a.
[12]Sabb. 25b.
[13]Meg. 27a.
[14]Yeb. 63a.
[15]Sotah 12a.
[16]Yeb. 63.
[17]Gen. R. 68.4.
[18]Sotah 12a.
[19]Yeb. 63.
[20]B. Metzia 59.
[21]Gitt. 90.
[22]Sanh. 29.
[23]Sanh. 22.
[24]Hosea 2:21f.
[25]Isa. 54:5.
[26]Jeremiah 2:2.
[27]David Mace, *Hebrew Marriage* (New York: Philosophical Library, 1953), p. 121 f.
[28]Miller Burrows, *The Basis of Israelite Marriage* (New Haven: American Oriental Society, 1938), p. 9. Johs Pedersen, *Israel* (London: Oxford University Press, 1926), Vol I-II, p. 70.
[29]I. Jacobson, *The Social Background of the Old Testament* (Cincinnati: Hebrew Union College Press, 1947), p. 49.
[30]1 Sam. 1:16; Lev. 18:18. Raphael Patai makes note that

"the very name by which a co-wife is called today in Arabic, *darrah,* is the same by which she was called in Hebrew in biblical times (*sarah*)." *Sex and Family in the Bible and the Middle East* (New York: Doubleday, 1959), p. 40.

[31]Lev. 18:8.

[32]Ex. 21: 7-11.

[33]Yeb. 65a.

[34]Ex. 21:7.

[35]Deut. 20:14.

[36]Ex. 21:2-11.

[37]Louis Epstein, "The Institution of Concubinage Among the Jews," *Proceedings of the American Academy for Jewish Research* (Philadelphia: Jewish Publication Society, 1935), VI, 155.

[38]*Dialogue,* 134.1: 141. 4.

[39]*Justinian Institute,* i. 10. 6.

[40]S. Zucrow, *Woman, Slaves, and the Ignorant in Rabbinic Literature* (Boston: The Stratford Company, 1932), p. 72.

[41]M. Mielziner, *The Jewish Law of Marriage and Divorce* (New York: Bloch Printing Company, 1901), p. 30.

[42]*Ibid.*, p. 32.

[43]Gen. 2:18-24.

[44]Gen. 4:23.

[45]R. H. Kennett, *Ancient Hebrew Social Life and Customs as Indicated in Law, Narrative, and Metaphor* (London: British Academy, 1933), p. 18.

[46]Jer. 3:8; Ez. 16:32.

[47]Prov. 12:4; Eccl. 9:9.

[48]M. Yeb. 2:9-10.

[49]A. Cowley (trans.), *Aramaic Papyri of the Fifth Century B.C.* (Oxford: Clarendon Press, 1923), pp. 6, 7, 9, 15.

[50]T. H. Gaster (trans.), *The Dead Sea Scriptures* (Garden City: Doubleday Anchor, 1957), p. 66.

[51]H. H. Rowley, *The Zadokite Fragments and the Dead Sea Scrolls* (Oxford: Basil Blackwell, 1952), p. 36.

[52]Jean Juster, *Les Juifs dans l'Empire romain* (Paris: Librairie Paul Guethner, 1914), II, p. 52.

[53]R. H. Charles, *Apocrypha and Pseudepigrapha of the Old Testament in English* (Oxford: Oxford University Press, 1913),

p. 105.

[54]G. F. Moore, *Judaism* (Cambridge: Harvard Press, 1944), II, p. 122; E. B. Gross, *The Hebrew Family* (Chicago: The University of Chicago Press, 1927), p. 210; E. Westermarck, *The History of Human Marriage* (London: The Macmillan Company, 1921), III, p. 41.

[55]Plato, *Symposium*, trans. P. B. Shelley, *Five Dialogues of Plato* (London: J. M. Dent and Sons, 1929), p. 35.

[56]David Daube, *The New Testament and Rabbinic Judaism* (London: University of London Press, 1956), p. 72.

[57]M. Grunwald, "Androgynos," *Jewish Encyclopedia* (New York: Funk and Wagnalls Company), I, p. 580.

[58]Gen. Rab. vii. 1.

[59]Yeb. 63a.

[60]Gen. Rab. v. 2.

[61]Gaster, *op. cit.*, p. 66.

[62]*On the Creation*, xxiv. 76.

[63]Charles Ryder Smith, *The Bible Doctrine of Womanhood* (London: The Epworth Press, 1923), p. 67.

[64]Emil Hirsch, "Asceticism," *Jewish Encyclopedia,* I, p. 166.

[65]Lev. 19:28; Deut. 14:1; 23:1.

[66]Louis Finkelstein, *The Pharisees* (Philadelphia: The Jewish Publication Society, 1940), Vol. 1, p. 43.

[67]*Antiquities,* xviii. 1.5.

[68]K. Kohler, "Essenes," *Jewish Encyclopedia,* V, p. 226.

[69]Millar Burrows, *The Dead Sea Scrolls* (New York: The Viking Press, 1955), p. 244.

[70]*Wisdom of Solomon,* 3:13-14.

[71]Moore, *op. cit.*, p. 264.

[72]W. G. Cole, *Sex and Love in the Bible* (New York: Association Press, 1959), pp. 53, 87.

[73]Yeb. 63b.

[74]Gen. Rab. xvii. 2.

[75]Yeb. 65b.

[76]Deut. 25:5-10; Gen. 38.

[77]Millar Burrows, "Levirate Marriage in Israel," *Journal of Biblical Literature* (Philadelphia: Society of Biblical Literature and Exegesis, 1940), LIX, p. 33.

[78]Judith 8:7.
[79]Yeb. 88; 113; 114b.
[80]Lev. 21:7.
[81]Lev. 21:7, 14.
[82]Lev. 22:13.
[83]Num. 30:9.
[84]Deut. 22:19, 29.
[85]Deut. 24:1-4.
[86]S. R. Driver, *Deuteronomy, The International Critical Commentary* (New York: Charles Scribner's Sons, 1895), p. 270. C. F. Keil and F. Delitzsch, *Pentateuch* (Edinburgh: T. and T. Clark, 1867), III, p. 416.
[87]Gitt. 9. 10.
[88]*Ibid.*
[89]*Ibid.*
[90]Mielziner, *op. cit.*, p. 119, n. 1.
[91]Robert Gordis, "The Jewish Concept of Marriage," *Judaism* (New York: American Jewish Congress, 1953), II, p. 229.
[92]*Antiquities of the Jews,* iv. 8. 23.
[93]*The Special Laws,* iii. 5. 30.
[94]Ket. 3:4-5.
[95]Mal. 2:14-16.
[96]Gen. Rab. xvii. 3.
[97]Jacobson, *op. cit.*, p. 83; Pederson, *op. cit.*, p. 71.
[98]M. Yeb. 6:6; Yeb. 64a.
[99]J. Keth. 5:7.
[100]Yeb. 65b.
[101]Pederson, *op. cit.*, p. 370.
[102]Ex. 20:14; Deut. 5:18.
[103]W. Kornfeld, "L'adultère dans l'Orient antique," *Revue Biblique* (Paris: Librairie Lecoffre, 1950), LVII, 108.
[104]Eccus. 23:23-27.
[105]Sotah 5b.
[106]Sanh. 74a.
[107]Deut. 22:22; Lev. 20:10. For similar laws, see the Code of Hammurabi 129; Assyrian Code i. 13; Hittite Code 197.
[108]Salo Baron, *A Social and Religious History of the Jews* (New York: Columbia University, 1952), II, 222.

[109]Abrahams, *Studies in Pharisaism and the Gospels* (Cambridge: University Press, 1917), p. 73.
[110]*Apion,* ii. 5.
[111]Sanh. 41a.
[112]John 8:1-11.
[113]Num. 5:11-31; M. Sotah 1:1.
[114]M. Sotah 9:9.
[115]M. Keth. 3:4-5; Sanh. 52b; J. Sotah 1. 1. 16b.
[116]Louis Epstein, *The Jewish Marriage Contract* (New York: Jewish Theological Seminary, 1927), p. 210.
[117]David Amram, *The Jewish Law of Divorce* (Philadelphia: Edward Stern and Company, 1896), p. 54.
[118]*Antiquities,* xv. 7. 10; xviii. 5.4.
[119]*Ibid.*
[120]Keth. 110b.
[121]Ex. 21:7-11.
[122]M. Arak. 5:6.
[123]*Ibid.*
[124]Ex. 21:10.
[125]M. Keth. 5:6.
[126]M. Ned. 11:12.
[127]Yeb. 65.
[128]Num. 30:8-9.
[129]Ket. 72a.
[130]M. Ket. 7:2-5.
[131]M. Ket. 7:9-10.
[132]*Ibid.*
[133]*Ibid.*
[134]M. Ket. 5:8-9.
[135]Ket. 63a.
[136]M. Ket. 3:4-5.
[137]*On Special Laws,* iii. 14. 82.
[138]Ket. 110b.
[139]John Paterson, "Divorce and Desertion in the Old Testament," *The Journal of Biblical Literature* (Philadelphia: Society of Biblical Literature and Exegesis, 1927), p. 167.
[140]Ket. 30b.
[141]M. Gitt. 9:8.

[142]Gitt. 90b.
[143]*Ibid.*
[144]*Ibid.*
[145]Deut. 24:1.
[146]Isa. 50:1.
[147]C. H. Gordon, *The World of the Old Testament* (New York: Harper Brothers, 1958), pp. 229-230.
[148]M. Gitt. 9:3.
[149]Gitt. 66b.
[150]Gitt. 24a; 26a.
[151]Gitt. 19a; 26b.
[152]Gitt. 77a.
[153]Gitt. 7a; 64b.
[154]Baba Metzia 1:7.
[155]Gitt. 76b.
[156]Gen. Rab. 17:3.
[157]Shab. 14b.
[158]Epstein, *Marriage Contract*, p. 31.
[159]Gen. 34:11-12.
[160]Gen. 24:53.
[161]Ex. 22:15-16.
[162]Amram, *op. cit.*, p. 113.
[163]M. Ket. 7:6.
[164]*Ibid.*
[165]Deut. 22:28-29.
[166]*Ibid.*
[167]M. Yeb. 4:2.
[168]M. Ket. 4:9.
[169]Deut. 24:3.
[170]*On Special Laws*, iii. 3. 28.
[171]M. Yeb. 4:2.
[172]M Sotah 2:6.
[173]M. Gitt. 4:7.
[174]M. Gitt. 4:11.
[175]M. Gitt. 4:7.
[176]M. Baba B. 10:9.
[177]Arak. 6:1.
[178]M. Gitt. 4:7.

[179]M. Yeb. 2:9.
[180]Lev. 21:7.
[181]*On Special Laws,* i. 108.
[182]Yeb. 41.
[183]Yeb. 42.
[184]Extra-marital relations with another's wife were prohibited, but relations with a single woman were evaluated differently since in a polygamous society she was a potential wife.
[185]*Apion,* ii. 24. 199.
[186]Yoma 29a.
[187]Kid. 50b.
[188]Ber. 43b.
[189]Erub. 18b.
[190]Kid. 81a; Ber. 24a.
[191]M. Aboth 2:7.
[192]Yeb. 105b. See Juster, *op. cit.,* II. p. 54; Baron, *op. cit.,* II, p. 219.
[193]Baron, *op. cit.,* II, p. 219.
[194]Kid. 29b.
[195]Eccus. 26: 10-12.
[196]Nid. 13b.
[197]Deut. 22:28-29.
[198]C. H. Gordon, "The Status of Women Reflected in the Nuzi Tablets," *Zeitschrift für Assyriologie* (1936), N. T. IX, p. 148.
[199]Gen. 38.
[200]Jos. 2.
[201]Jud. 16.
[202]Pes. 113b.
[203]Prov. 2:16-19; 5:1-27; Eccus. 9:3-9; 19:2; 26:9.
[204]P. Humbert, "La femme étrangère du Livre des Proverbs," *Revue des études sémitiques,* XIII (Paris, 1937), p. 64.
[205]*On Special Laws,* iii. 51.
[206]C. H. Toy, *Proverbs, The International Critical Commentary* (New York: Charles Scribner's Sons, 1899), p. 54.
[207]Finkelstein, *op. cit.,* p. 556.
[208]Baron, *op. cit.,* II, p. 225.
[209]M. Sotah 9:9.
[210]Yoma 19b.

[211]*On Joseph*, 43.
[212]Erub. 21b.
[213]M. Ket. 3:1-2.
[214]Epstein, *Sex Laws*, p. 148.

CHAPTER IV

MARRIAGE AND DIVORCE IN THE NEW TESTAMENT

Christianity did not begin in a vacuum. Its roots were deep in the soil of Judaism; its branches reached out into the Gentile world. Although the church's task was to influence its environment, it could not escape being influenced. Its attitude toward marriage and divorce was influenced by Jewish and Roman backgrounds. This chapter will be concerned with the interaction of these forces upon the message of Jesus and his disciples as exemplified in the New Testament.

MARRIAGE

Marriage among the early Christians, as among the Jews, was held in the highest regard. Despite the limited length of the New Testament and the diverse interests of the authors, there is considerable evidence that Christians believed marriage to be ordained by God and good in and of itself.

Object of Praise

The esteem in which marriage was held is indicated in every section of the New Testament canon. In the Gospels it should not be overlooked that Jesus attended and performed his first sign at the wedding in Cana.[1] Nor is the amount of space allotted to marriage and related subjects in the Sermon on the Mount insignificant.[2] Although there is no consensus as to all Jesus meant on this occasion, as shall be shown later, there can be no misunderstanding of his great respect for the institution of marriage. This is seen nowhere as clearly as in his use of the wedding metaphor in connection with his teaching about the kingdom. The kingdom is compared to a feast,[3] and to a royal marriage.[4] Jesus is the bridegroom, the disciples are the guests,[5] and John the Baptist is the "best man."[6] Jesus saw the origin of marriage in God's plan which existed from creation.[7] In fact, his estimate was so high that some of his apostles viewed marriage with apprehension.[8]

The disciples of Jesus who wrote the New Testament shared his respect for the institution. This is indicated not only by the Gospel writers' decision to record Jesus' teaching on the subject, but also their discussion of the subject in the Epistles. It is Paul, the most prolific writer, who is the most comprehensive in dealing with marriage. The most detailed regulations for the conjugal relation are given by him in the seventh chapter of First Corinthians. Marriage, at least for those who have been widowed and remarried, is "in the Lord."[9] In another place, he specifically says that it is possible to "take a wife . . . in honor and holiness."[10] The supreme example, however, of Paul's appreciation of marriage is his use of it as a figure to describe the church's relationship to Christ. He reminds the Corinthian church that they have been betrothed to Christ as "a pure bride to her one husband."[11] This idea is spelled out more completely in the fifth chapter of Ephesians. The metaphor of marriage as a description of the relationship between God and Israel is a common one in Judaism;[12] but here Jesus, and not God, is the bridegroom. Piper[13] sees four important parallels in verses 23-33 between the relationship of Christ and the church and the relationship between husband and wife. They are: (a) a unity that is like a sex unity; (b) a love that sin cannot set aside; (c) the church's reception of spiritual gifts as a wife receives the man's seed; and (d) the inability of the two to be thought of separately. There are other passages which are no less emphatic in their praise of matrimony. In the Pastoral Epistles it is stated that "everything created by God is good, and nothing is to be rejected."[14] To this the author of Hebrews adds, "Let marriage be held in honor among all, and let the marriage bed be undefiled."[15] There is ample evidence that marriage was held in honor and practiced by the followers of Jesus.[16]

Form of Marriage

There can be little doubt that the form of marriage envisioned in the New Testament is that of monogamy. Although there are no direct statements on the subject, general passages seem to exclude the idea of polygamy. It must be admitted that polygamy was technically a possibility among the Jews of Jesus' time. That this was also possible among the Jewish Christians is unlikely in the light of Mark 10:11 where Jesus speaks of a man committing adultery "against her," that is, one's wife. This idea of committing adultery against a wife is impossible in polygamous societies.[17] Similar evidence from Jesus is recorded in Matthew where instructions are given for a man to leave his parents and cleave to his wife with the result that the two become "one flesh."[18] As Daube points out, this quotation of Genesis 2:24 is from the Septuagint.[19] The Hebrew text supported by the Targum and Jubilees 3:7 does not have the word "two," but merely, "and they shall become one flesh." Daube suggests that it was added in the Septuagint "in order to enjoin monogamy, considered as the more civilized practice by the Greeks."[20] There are also two Pauline passages which imply monogamy. The first refers to each man having his own wife and each wife her own man as a safeguard against fornication.[21] The second passage deals with authority and says that Christ is head of the church as the husband is head of the wife.[22] In contrast with these, the clearest passage reflecting a polygamous situation is found in the Pastoral Epistles. In discussing the qualification for a bishop, it is stated that he must be the "husband of one wife" (μῖας γυναικὸς ἄνδρα).[23] This might suggest that some Christians had a plurality of wives and therefore would be disqualified as bishops. What renders this unlikely is the occurrence in the same context of the phrase "wife of one husband" (ἑνὸς ἀνδρὸς γυνή) as a qualification for the enrollment of widows in the church.[24] If the phrase in reference to bishops excludes polygamy, the phrase in reference to widows must prohibit polyandry. Polyandry, however, was never practiced in the Roman world. These phrases must, then, refer either to digamy or divorce.[25]

Depreciation of Marriage

That the early church esteemed marriage is true, but it is not the complete picture. Existing side by side with passages which extol matrimony are other passages which seemingly extol celibacy. These scriptural references are related either to the idea of sexual abstinence or digamy.

Abstinence.—There are several sayings of Jesus that can be taken as favoring the celibate state. Perhaps the best known remark is in regard to those who are "eunuchs for the sake of the Kingdom of Heaven."[26] The same idea is expressed elsewhere by Jesus' statement of the possibility of men leaving their wives for the sake of the Kingdom.[27] These remarks, however, are not made in a spirit of asceticism based on a thoroughgoing dualism.

Jesus is certainly not advocating emasculation. The Jews made a distinction between eunuchs from birth and those made so by men; to this Jesus adds a third group—voluntary eunuchs.[28] As Manson indicates, the very idea of emasculation would be against the whole sentiment of Judaism.[29] Jesus' words were understood by the church following the New Testament period to indicate celibacy. Thus Clement of Alexandria says that true eunuchs are not those who cannot lust, but those who will not lust.[30] "Jesus requires not asceticism," Bultmann says, "he requires only the strength for sacrifice."[31] What Jesus is saying is that marriage and family, although ordained by God, can leave a person insensible to the message of the Kingdom. Families hindered people in the days of Noah and Lot and could do so again. The Kingdom deserves first-class loyalty and one cannot be a disciple if this loyalty is given to anything else, even marriage. This voluntary celibacy was not universally applicable. Jesus warned, "Not all men can receive this precept, but only those to whom it is given."[32] That Jesus himself did not marry is not an indication of a personal prejudice against matrimony, for, while he did not take a wife, he did take a church.[33] Jesus was, in fact, so far from being a thoroughgoing advocate of abstinence that the supporters of celibacy found it necessary to attribute statements favorable to their position to him in the apocryphal gospels.[34]

Outside of the Gospels, the most important passages supporting celibacy are found in the opening and closing verses of the seventh chapter of I Corinthians. The best policy, Paul says, is for a man "not to touch a woman."[35] This expression is an euphemism for sexual relations as is clearly indicated by use of it in the Septuagint.[36] The context makes it clear that this advice on Paul's part is not to be taken as an absolute precept. The celibate state, the apostle thought, would free a person from the anxiety relating to family matters (vs. 33) and hence would permit complete devotion to the Lord's work (vs. 32). This would make for a happier condition in general for the Christian (vs. 40). It is also clear that celibacy is "good" in the apostle's mind because of two factors. First, celibacy is good in the light of the "impending distress" (vs. 26). The distress is described as a tribulation in the flesh (vs. 28), a shortened time (vs. 29), and a passing away of the form of the world (vs. 31). This is to say that the belief in the early return of Christ and the consummation of the world influenced Paul's view of marriage.[37] The second factor which seemed to him to make celibacy the preferred state is that it is a gift of God (vs. 7). Not everyone had this gift, Paul recognized, and so to those to whom it was not given marriage was without sin (vss. 28, 36). In fact, marriage must also be a "good" because it guards one against the sin of fornication (vs. 2) and keeps one from burning (vs. 9). It must be understood therefore, that when Paul wrote that celibacy was "good," he was not necessarily suggesting that marriage was bad. He was really saying what Jesus had said before him; namely, that the Kingdom of God takes precedence over everything else.

The closing verses of the seventh chapter of First Corinthians in the English text also seem to support celibacy.[38] There is a considerable difference between the rendering of this passage in translations, although there is no textual variant. It appears in the King James Version and the Revised Standard Version, respectively, as follows:

> But if any man think that he behaveth himself uncomely toward his virgin, if she pass the flower of her age, and need so require, let him do what he will, he sinneth not; let them marry. Nevertheless he that standeth steadfast in his heart, having no necessity, but hath power over his own will, and hath so decreed in his heart that he will keep his virgin, doeth well. So then he that giveth her in marriage doeth well; but he that giveth her not in marriage doeth better.

> If anyone thinks that he is not behaving properly toward his betrothed, if his passions are strong, and it has to be, let them do as he wishes; let them marry —it is no sin. But whoever is firmly established in his heart, being under no necessity but having his desire under control, and has determined this in his heart, to keep her as his betrothed, he will do well. So that he who marries his betrothed does well; and he who refrains from marriage will do better.

The King James Version, which is followed by the American Standard, interprets this paragraph as instructions given to a father concerning his virgin daughter. This rendering is not without its supporters.[39] Key to this interpretation is γαμίζω which can only be interpreted, so the advocates say, as "given in marriage." The relationship then would have to be either that of a father and his daughter, or a guardian and his ward, or a master and a slave. There are several difficulties with this position. The phrase "let them marry" (vs. 37) would suddenly introduce the fiance into the text for the first time. The father would awkwardly be referring to "his virgin" rather than "his daughter." And if the daughter has already passed the age of marriage, it seems strange that the father is suffering all the anguish of the inner struggle. If the relationship was that of guardian and ward or master and slave, then these difficulties would be solved. It seems doubtful, however, that Paul would discuss such a specialized subject in such a general way.

The interpretation reflected in the Revised Version hinges upon reading γαμίζω as if it were γαμέω; that is, reading "marry" rather than "give in marriage." In justification for this is the fact that in later Greek there was a tendency for ιζω verbs to lose their causative significance. Thus, Arndt-Gingrich gives it as a possible translation for γαμίζω.[40] This position would be stronger if there were an example of this particular verb used without the causative quality. Its supporters, therefore, are forced to rely on analogy between γαμίζω and other ιζω verbs. Having assumed this reading, there are several possible meanings for the text. Paul could have had in mind engaged couples who finally decided to live celibate lives. This would especially be attractive if the couple were from a Jewish background where engagement was as binding as matrimony. Or perhaps Paul had reference to "spiritual marriages" in which couples lived sexless lives. While most of the evidence for such platonic unions is much later, there are those who see the beginning of the practice in the Corinthian church.[41] Neither the interpretation of the King James Version nor that of the Revised Standard is completely free of difficulty; Moffatt is correct, however, in saying that the latter position has the lesser difficulty.[42]

Outside the Gospels and the Pauline corpus, there are few New Testament passages pertaining to celibacy. In Acts, there is the mention of the virgin daughters of Philip, but they are cited without comment.[43] The passage that comes the closest to suggesting that sex itself is evil is Revelation 14:4 in which the author speaks of men who have "not defiled themselves with women." Whatever explanation there may be for this, it seems inconsistent for the author to exalt virginity in one place and in other places speak of the marriage of the Lamb.[44]

Digamy.—There is some indication that the second century church's prejudice against digamy, that is, a second marriage after the death of the original mate, was beginning to develop during the apostolic period. The Gospels are silent concerning Jesus' attitude toward digamy. The most relevant comment was made when the

Sadducees came to him with the hypothetical case of the woman who had married seven brothers. This was, of course, an allusion to the practice of *levirate* marriage. It is clear that this institution had ceased to exist before the time of Christ.[45] Jesus merely replied that in the afterlife marriage as an institution will no longer exist, without commenting upon the validity of the hypothetical question.

Paul, in contrast to Jesus, seems to be concerned about digamy. Twice, once in Romans[46] and again in First Corinthians,[47] Paul states that a marital union exists only as long as physical life. When one partner dies, the surviving mate is free. This is in agreement with what Jesus says about marriage not transcending this life. Judaism as we have seen, encouraged remarriage.[48] Paul probably reflects this view, except he feels that it could be a disadvantage[49] and limits such marriage of Christians to other Christians.[50] There are some scholars who feel that the phrase, "in the Lord," does not mean marry only a Christian.[51] The second group of passages which have some bearing on digamy are found in the Pastoral Epistles. There it is stated that remarriage could remove a widow from the list of church-supported widows.[52] Also in the qualifications of elders or bishops and deacons, it is stated that they must be a "one-woman man" (μῖας γυναικὸς ἄνδρα); likewise, it is stated that a widow on the church's list must be a "one-man woman" (ἑνὸς ἀνδρὸς γυνή). There is no unanimity concerning the interpretation of the Greek word. The suggested interpretations include: (1) that this passage prohibits polygamy,[53] (2) that it requires a man to be married in order to hold the office of elder,[54] (3) that he be married and undivorced, i.e., a prohibition against an elder being a divorced man,[55] and (4) that it prohibits a person remarrying after the death of the first mate. Spicq[56] and Watkins[57] hold this latter position. It would seem that the determinative factor in the interpretation of the passage about elders is the fact that the same word, with the appropriate change of sex, is also used concerning widows. Since, in First Timothy, the discussion of the widows is to be considered in light of their being added to the relief rolls of the church, and since polyandry was not practiced, it seems impossible to understand this as a prohibition against polygamy. Neither does it seem reasonable to believe that it was included primarily to suggest that the person must be married. In all likelihood, the person would be married, since the passage goes on to mention the elder's family. In the case of widows it seems self-evident they would have been married.The two most likely interpretations, therefore, are that it is either to prohibit a divorced person from holding office or being on the church roll; or, it is the prohibition of the same for digamists. J. B. Frey, in his survey of μονάνδρος and the Latin equivalent *univira* on epitaphs, suggests that its primary meaning was concerning the undivorced. He concludes: "In a dozen pagan epitaphs in which the word *univira* occurs, nine are put there by surviving husbands."[58]

DIVORCE

While those who accepted Christianity accepted the ethical teachings of the new faith, they still had the problem of living with their own human nature and the pagan environment in which they found themselves. Divorce, therefore, was a problem for them regardless of the exalted nature they gave to the institution of marriage. Divorce was a common phenomenon in both the Hellenistic and Jewish world. There is indication from the biblical record that it was also a serious concern in the Christian community.

Grounds for Divorce

A survey of the Scriptures indicates that several factors are related to divorce. The passages may be catalogued as follows: (1) passages which suggest there is no possibility of divorce; (2) passages which seem to indicate that "unchastity" (πορνεία) is the only ground for divorce; and (3) passages which seem to suggest that an exception is made in the case of mixed marriages between Christians and non-believers (this is commonly called the Pauline Privilege). We shall look at each in turn.

No exception.—The primary passage suggesting the impossibility of divorce is the pericope of Mark 10:2-12.

> And the Pharisees came up and in order to test him asked, "Is it lawful for a man to divorce his wife?" He answered them, "What did Moses com-

> mand you?" They said, "Moses allowed a man to write a certificate of divorce, and to put her away." But Jesus said to them, "For your hardness of heart he wrote you this commandment. But from the beginning of creation, 'God made them male and female. For this reason a man shall leave his father and mother and be joined to his wife, and the two shall become one.' So they are not longer two but one. What therefore, God has joined together, let not man put asunder." And in the house the disciples asked him again about this matter. And he said to them, "Whoever divorces his wife and marries another, commits adultery against her; and if she divorces her husband and marries another, she commits adultery."

The parallel passage in Luke 16:18 simply says:

> Everyone who divorces his wife and marries another commits adultery, and he who marries a woman divorced from her husband commits adultery.

In seeking to trap Jesus, the Pharisees phrased a question concerning marriage. The question was, "Is it lawful for a man to divorce his wife?" Jesus understood their query as a legal matter and referred them to the law of Moses. Moses' bill of divorcement was only a temporary concession and was out of harmony with the original purpose of marriage as given in the creation stories. The concept of the two becoming one flesh would not only prohibit polygamy, as has been indicated,[59] but also divorce. The force of Jesus' reply would be that it is wrong for a man to divorce his wife. There are three passages outside the Gospels that lend support to this position. The first is found in First Corinthians where Paul instructs:

> To the married I give charge, not I but the Lord, that the wife should not separate from her husband (but if she does, let her remain single or else be reconciled to her husband)—and that the husband should not divorce his wife.[60]

The importance of this passage is that Paul, in quoting Jesus on the subject, does not include the exception clause. The two other passages, similar in nature, are found respectively in First Corinthians and Romans.

> A wife is bound to her husband as long as he lives. If the husband dies, she is free to be married to whom she wishes, only in the Lord.[61] Do you know, brethren—for I am speaking to those who know the law—that the law is binding on a person only during his life? Thus a married woman is bound by law to her husband as long as he lives; but if her husband dies she is discharged from the law concerning the husband. Accordingly, she will be called an adulteress if she lives with another man while her husband is alive. But if her husband dies she is free from that law, and if she marries another man she is not an adulteress.[62]

The significance of these passages is that Paul envisions only an either/or position; either a couple are married until death, or there is adultery. Some scholars find here the basic New Testament doctrine of the indissolubility of marriage.[63] The chief objection to the "no exception" position is the verses in Matthew's gospel which speak specifically of an exception—adultery (πορνεία).

> But I say to you that everyone who divorces his wife, except on the grounds of unchastity, makes her an adulteress; and whoever marries a divorced woman commits adultery. [64]
>
> And I say to you: whoever divorces his wife, except for unchastity, and marries another, commits adultery.[65]

In the long history of exegesis these two passages have been treated by the fertile imaginations of scholars in a wide variety of ways. While there have been many adaptations, there are only a few basic approaches.

Separation.—Perhaps the most frequent explanation of the passages in Matthew concerns the meaning of the word "divorces." Some who maintain the primacy of the Markan statement do so by advocating that "divorces" means simply to separate from bed and board without the right of remarriage.[66] The greatest problem with this interpretation is the strained meaning which must be given to "divorce" (ἀπολύειν, literally "to dismiss"). In the first part of the context the word must mean freedom to remarry; in the second part it is taken to mean "separation." Separation in the modern sense of the word was unknown to the Jews who certainly would not have understood this new idea.[67] It is clear that the Pharisees who asked the question in Matthew 19:9 were doing so against the background of Deuteronomy 24:1 which plainly presents the right to remarry. For Jesus to answer their question by saying that a simple separation is legal seems unintelligible. The idea of separation, if it were granted, would not completely solve the problem, for Matthew 19:9 implies the right of one who divorces his mate on the grounds of unchastity to remarry, which would obviously be impossible if Jesus were only granting the right of separation.

Textual Variant.—The most important verse in the New Testament concerning divorce, according to Watkins, [68] is Matthew 19:9 which includes the implied right to remarry. It so happens that the difficulty it presents to those who maintain the indissolubility of marriage is nullified by a textual variant. The two readings are:

Accepted: μὴ ἐπί πορνεία καὶ γαμήσῃ ἄλλην μοιχᾶται
"except for unchastity and marries another, commits adultery"

Variant: παρεκτὸς λόγου πορνείας ποιεῖ αὐτὴν μοιχευθῆναι
"except for the cause of unchastity makes her an adulteress"

The variant reading would bring Matthew 19:9 into exact agreement with 5:32 for it only discusses the situation when a non-adulterous wife is put away with the result being the husband "makes her an adulteress." The question remains as to which reading represents the genuine text. For this answer we must turn to textual criticism.

In support of the presently accepted text is an impressive array including the Codex Sinaiticus plus twelve other Uncials, almost all other Greek texts, the Old Latin texts, and most of the translations. While the number of manuscripts should not be the deciding factor, they would require some explanation for their rejection. In fact it is more plausible to explain the existence of the variant reading, assuming it spurious, than the origin of the currently accepted text. The variant can be explained as an attempt to harmonize Matthew 19:9 with the other passages. If the variant is genuine, all the passages would agree; however, the appearance of the dissimilar reading would be difficult to explain.

The strongest support for the variant reading comes from the Codex Vaticanus. While this witness cannot be dismissed lightly, the weight it carries can be better ascertained when the variant reading is divided into its two clauses. The first half, παρεκτὸς λόγου πορνείας, is supported not only by the Codex Vaticanus, but also by the Codex Bezae, eight cursives including 1 and 33, and several Old Latin manuscripts. When the second half of the reading is considered, that is, ποιεῖ ἀυτῆν μοιχευθῆναι, the support that "B" received is not as strong as in the first phrases. Here Codex Bezae supports Sinaiticus as do several of the Old Latin manuscripts. This is to say that the support for the former half of the variant reading is stronger than for the latter half. It is this latter half, ποιεῖ ἀυτὴν μοιχενθῆναι ("makes her an adulteress"), that is crucial. The first half of the variation is easily explained as an assimilation to the words of Matthew 5:32. It has been suggested that the absence of καί γαμήσῃ ἄλλην ("and shall marry another") has dropped out of some manuscripts because of *homoitheleuten*, that is, the repetition of the word μοιχᾶται in the text.[65]

The most serious attempt to defend the variant reading as genuine comes from Burton Scott Easton.[70] In addition to appealing to the authority of the Codex Vaticanus, Easton asserts that the crucial matter is the non-Jewish statement that a married man can commit adultery. This statement of the accepted text Easton explains on the grounds that non-Jews transcribed the Gospels and would be more likely to change a Jewish idea into a Greek one. Easton further believes that Matthew took the non-Jewish statement from Q and corrected it in 5:32 and that he would surely solve the problem in the same way in 19:9. The statement that Greeks would be more prone to change Jewish ideas into Greek rather than vice versa might be true. But the textual variant could be accounted for just as easily by assimilation to 5:32 without regard to modes of expression. It is possible to start from the non-Jewish expression represented by Mark 10:2-12 and argue in the opposite direction from Easton, that is, because of its non-Jewish characteristics it is inferior to the Matthean passages.[71] The variant reading finds strongest support, however, in Origen. In his *Commentary on Saint Matthew*, he quotes the variant text and appears to know nothing of the standard text.[72] Clement of Alexandria once quotes a passage concerning divorce and adultery, but apparently quotes from memory, with the result that it is uncertain which passage he had in mind.[73] In another place, however, it is certain that he is familiar with the standard text of Matthew 19:9.[74] Cirlot[75] also finds support in Tertullian's reply to Marcion's charge that the God of the Old Testament is different from the God of the New, since one permitted divorce and the other did not. Tertullian's response is that divorce is not absolutely prohibited.[76] Tertullian's task, so Cirlot advocates, would have been far easier had he quoted Matthew 19:9; that he did not is an indication that the accepted text was not in his Bible. While some scholars accept the variant reading or dismiss the text as "so corrupt that it cannot reasonably be depended on to establish any theory,"[77] they do so against the weight of textual material in favor of the accepted text. The unanimity of the critical editors of the Greek text, namely Tischendorf, Westcott and Hort, von Soden, Nestle, and Souter, in preference for the standard reading can be taken as scholarly affirmation of its correctness.

Interpolation.— The exception clause is held by many scholars, especially Protestants, to be an interpolation at the hand either of Matthew himself,[78] or a later editor.[79] This was deemed necessary to accommodate the "hard saying" to the frailty of human nature,[80] or perhaps to accommodate the practice of divorce to the Jewish law.[81] This position is reached, however, without regard to the sound principles of textual criticism. There is no problem textually as far as the exception clause is concerned. The Matthean passages are reflected by many of the Fathers.[82] On the basis of textual history many scholars,[83] both Catholics and Protestants, reject the interpolation view. The grounds, therefore, upon which the clause is rejected are theological rather than textual. While it would doubtless be of some advantage to know whether the exception clause was actually spoken by Jesus, it is not crucial. Whatever the origin of the exception clause, it represents an opinion in the Ante-Nicene church and therefore deserves consideration.

Prenuptial Unchastity.—A few scholars[84] have held the position that "except for unchastity" refers to premarital sexual relations. The Matthean passages, therefore, would not touch the matter of divorce for adultery. Only if a man discovered his bride not to be a virgin could he put her away. The fact is that there is a similar law in the Old Testament favoring this interpretation. In Deuteronomy a man who so suspects his bride is instructed:

> . . . if the thing is not true, that the tokens of virginity were not found in the young woman, then they shall bring out the young woman to the door of her father's house, and the men of her city shall stone her to death with stones, because she has wrought folly in Israel by playing the harlot in her father's house; so you shall purge the evil from the midst of you.[85]

There is considerable evidence against this view, however. In the first place, while the word πορνεία can mean prenuptial unchastity, it usually has a much broader meaning. In the LXX version of Hosea 2:4-7 both "adultery" (μοιχεία) and "fornication" (πορνεία) are used in relation to the prophet's wife, Gomer. Certainly the word can be used for adultery.[86] Even more important is the fact that this idea is completely missing from the Fathers. If Jesus were referring to prenuptial unchastity, it is singular that the church so completely failed to grasp his message.[87]

Temporary Concession.—According to this view, the exception clause does permit the divorcing of an unfaithful mate but it is a permission given only to the Jews of Jesus' day.[88] This has the advantage of keeping the most apparent meaning of the exception clause and at the same time reconciling it to all else written about divorce in the New Testament. If the words of Jesus were only meant for the Jews, then it is consistent that they do not appear in the Gentile-oriented gospels of Mark and Luke nor in the writings of Paul. This solution is possible in the context of Matthew 19:9 where the Jews in reality are asking Jesus to choose between two rabbinical interpretations. The force of his words would then be, "As long as the law of Moses is in effect, the only grounds for divorce is adultery." This is impossible, however, in the context of Matthew 5:32. There the context contains the Sermon on the Mount, and specific contrast is made to the old law. For this view to be intelligible in the latter passage, it would have to presuppose that "divorce" refers to separations in Jesus' new teaching while the same word refers to "divorce with the right to remarry" in his stating of the Mosaic law in the previous verse.

Preterition.—Another possible interpretation is termed "preteritive" because it envisions Jesus as passing over rather than focusing attention on adultery. Augustine was apparently the first to suggest this concept.

> "Why, then," you ask, "did the Lord insert the ground of immorality? Why does He not say, in a general way: Whoever puts away his wife and marries another commits adultery, if he also is an adulterer who remarries after he puts away an unfaithful spouse?" I believe the Lord did not speak thus because He wished to mention what is more important. For, who denies that in each case, the adultery is greater, if another wife is taken after one who had committed no fornication has been put away, than if an unfaithful wife is put away and then another taken?[89]

The idea on which this view is developed is that the exception clause is an exception to the entire sentence and not simply to the verb. A precise explanation is made by Lehmkuhl.

> Grammatically, the clause in St. Matthew may modify one member of the sentence (that which refers to the putting away of the wife) without applying to the following member (the remarriage of the other), though we must admit that the construction is a little harsh.[90]

This interpretation has much in its favor, not the least of which is its simplicity and lack of strain upon the actual words. It is grammatically possible to take the exception as pertaining to the entire sentence. Such use of ἐι μή ("except") occurs in the New Testament in Matthew 12:4, Romans 14:14, and Galatians 1:19. The Matthean passage reads:

> . . . how he entered into the house of God and ate the bread of the Presence, which it was not lawful for him to eat nor for those who were with him, but only (ἐι μή) for the priests?[91]

The force of the divorce passage would become "Whoever puts away his wife commits adultery (πορνεία)—only, a man may put away his wife for adultery (πορνεία)." An impressive list of scholars accept the preteritive position.[92] The position is not without difficulty, however. An obvious question has been raised by Vawter, "But why should the Lord bring up the question of πορνεία at all, if he does so only to bypass it?"[93] Two replies have been made to this question. Augustine, who took πορνεία as adultery, anticipated the problem by asserting Jesus raised the issue to emphasize the greater crime of putting away a woman for something less than adultery.[94] Interestingly enough, such a view would make subtlety a method of emphasis. The second answer is presented by Lagrange. In his commentary on Matthew he suggests that Jesus taught separation because the Law of Moses required the adulteress to be stoned. That is, rather than place a disciple in the position of bringing about the death of his adulterous mate, he is merely to withdraw from the guilty one.[95] This interpretation assumes that the death penalty for adultery was still in effect during Jesus' day. There is general agreement, however, that the death penalty was no longer applicable during the Common Era.[96] Another difficulty is felt from a grammatical standpoint. Murray[97] has noted a characteristic in the other passages in the New Testament where the exception applies to the whole proposition. In every other case a complete general statement is made and then an exception to its completeness is added. In the case under consideration the exception is inserted before the statement is finished. Thus analogy is also against considering these passages in the preteritive sense.

Correction.—This view, which is given the name "Interpretative Interpretation" by Vawter,[98] presents Jesus as giving a corrected interpretation of the Deuteronomic teaching on divorce. The Jews believed that the Law of Moses permitted remarriage after divorce, but this understanding is faulty and it is corrected by Jesus. The fullest presentation of this position occurs in the writing of Francis Gigot:

> It is the authoritative teaching of One who has come "not to destroy but to fulfill" the Law, by declaring solemnly to his disciples that even the very highest apparent ground (viz., conjugal unfaithfulness) for divorce, is but a condition which makes lawful the permanent separation of husband and wife.[99]

The author views Moses' decree concerning the bill of divorce as really a deterrent to divorce which Moses considered a moral evil. Jesus in the absolute prohibition of divorce is demanding "a righteousness higher than the one enforced by the traditional saying of His opponents."[100] The basis for this interpretation is the passage in Deuteronomy. The key passage is verse four. Having discussed the writing of the bill of divorce for "some indecency," the text continues:

> . . . then her former husband, who sent her away, may not take her again to be his wife, after she has been defiled; for that is an abomination before the Lord, and you shall not bring guilt upon the land which the Lord your God gives you for an inheritance.[101]

Gigot's point is that the divorced woman is referred to in this verse as one who is "defiled" by the second marriage. This indicates, he concludes, that a wife who is put away by means of a bill because of adultery is not free to remarry. From this the idea is advanced that Matthew 5:32 is parallel to the Deuteronomy passage. "Commits adultery" is parallel to "has been defiled," and "except for fornication" is equivalent to "some indecency." In this explanation what is needed to prove the point is assumed. The equation of "some indecency" *'erwat dabar* with "except for fornication" παρεκτὸς λόγου πορνείας is denied by two Catholic scholars, Vawter[102] and Bonsirven.[103]

The consequence of this interpretation is that it in

essence makes Jesus' answer an academic statement or requires a kind of interim law which is to be in effect until the Gospel becomes a reality. It would also have the effect of making the contrast between what was said in the Law of Moses and his new teaching in the Sermon on the Mount quite meaningless.

Inclusive.—The force of this interpretation is to make the passage in Matthew 19:9 have the meaning, "Whosoever puts away his wife—including putting her away for fornication—and marries another commits adultery." The basis for such a rendering is the phrase μή ἐπὶ πορνεία. Here, ἐπί is taken to mean "over and above," "outside (the case) of," while μή is taken to mean "not even." The resulting meaning is hence "even not outside the case of adultery." This is a popular solution among Catholic scholars.[104]

The greatest obstacle in the way of this solution is a linguistic one. There is nothing inherent in the word, ἐπί to suggest the meaning of "outside of." It is true, however, that ἐπί with the dative sometimes takes on the sense of *super* or *praeter*, but this is derived from the context. Such an example is seen in Second Corinthians:

> And besides our own comfort we rejoiced still more at the joy of Titus, because his mind has been set at rest by you all.[105]

In this and other examples in the New Testament,[106] however, this meaning of "outside of" comes from the sentence context and not from ἐπί by itself.[107]

In the phrase under consideration, μή ἐπὶ πορνεία,

the μή is understood according to this view as an elliptical negative with the meaning of "not even," with the "even" being supplied. There is nothing in the sentence, as there was not in the rendering of ἐπί, to suggest that this is the case. Even if this interpretation of Matthew be granted, there is still the problem of Matthew 5:32 which reads, instead of μή ἐπί πορνεία, παρεκτὸς λόγου . . . The attempt is therefore to render the passage "in addition to fornication" rather than "except on account of fornication." It is true that "except" can on some occasions mean "in addition to."

> I can say, "Without you, I have four companions," and mean, "I have four companions in addition to you," but you would conclude that "without" therefore means "in addition to," and that when I go to say, "without counting you," I mean, "in addition to counting you."[108]

Examples of this usage are to be found in the New Testament. Paul concludes his speech to Agrippa with the words παρεκτὸς τῶν δεσμῶν τούτων which must obviously have the sense "except these chains."[109] On another occasion Paul wrote, "And, apart from other things (χωρὶς τῶν παρεκτός), there is the daily pressure upon me of my anxiety for all the churches."[110] This translation is necessary because the "other things" which have been excluded have already been mentioned in the previous verses.

> Three times I have been beaten with rods; once I was stoned. Three times I have been shipwrecked; a

night and a day I have been adrift at sea; on frequent journeys, in danger from rivers, danger from robbers, danger from my own people . . .[111]

It seems highly improbable that in both the Matthean passages the Evangelist would have gone to such lengths and with such grammatical involvement to include πορνεία in the category of inadequate reasons for divorce. As Holzmeister[112] has observed, if this had been Matthew's purpose, he could have achieved this end by merely adding a simple καί, καὶ ἐπὶ λόγου πορνείας, and there would have been no possibility for misunderstanding his intent.

Illegal Wife.—The position that Jesus was referring to a false or illegal wife enjoys considerable popularity in Catholic circles[113] and it is not without Protestant support.[114] This interpretation is built upon one of the precepts of the Law of Moses dealing with prohibited marriages. In Leviticus 18:7-18, the degrees of consanguinity and affinity which determine incestuous marriages are listed. These prohibited unions were called *zenout* "prostitution," in post-biblical Jewish thought.[115] The women who participated in such marriages were called prostitutes (*zona*). Maimonides considered incestuous marriages, that is, marriages to a pagan, marriages to proselytes discriminated against in Deuteronomy 23, and improper priestly marriages mentioned in Leviticus 21 as prostitution.[116] Such unions within the prohibited degrees of Leviticus 18 were considered void. The second phase of the argument is the equating of *zenout* with πορνεία. That πορνεία can refer to prohibited marriages is suggested by the Apostolic Decree related in the book of Acts.

> For it seemed good to the Holy Spirit and to us to lay upon you no greater burden than these necessary things: that you abstain from what has been sacrificed to idols and from blood and from what is strangled and from unchastity.[117]

This passage, which deals with the minimum Jewish requirements imposed upon gentile Christians, has provided some difficulties because it mentions sexual purity as a minimum requirement. This position, which makes πορνεία equivalent for a marriage within the Levitical prohibition, makes the problem disappear and fits in well with the other Jewish requirements of the decree. A similarly suggestive passage is from Paul's Corinthian correspondence. In the first letter he refers to a brother who was living with his father's wife by employing the word πορνεία.[118] Here πορνεία clearly stands for incest, that is, a relationship within the prohibited degree. This also would explain the Hebrew author's description of Esau as a fornicator (πόρνος),[119] while the account in Genesis merely indicates that he married a non-Jewish woman.[120]

There are several advantages to this position which would render the substance of the exception clause as "whoever dismisses his wife, except in those cases which are prohibited unions causes her to commit adultery." The greatest asset is that it eliminates any apparent contradiction between the recorded sayings of Jesus. It also follows the most common grammatical understanding of the passages under consideration.

There are, however, weighty objections against such an interpretation. First, there seems to be some apparent difficulty in justifying such exegesis in the light of the larger context. If this is the accepted idea, then in Matthew 19:9 Jesus introduces a subject about which there would be no disagreement. In the context of Matthew 5:32 it makes Jesus, in the Sermon on the Mount, give instruction about the perpetuation of the Levitical law, while everywhere else he is concerned with the perfection of that law. Also Vawter asks, "To what purpose, moreover, would our Lord have confirmed the invalidity of *zenout*-marriages?"[121] He suggests that it is not to make the Levitical instruction binding on the church. He further appeals to the very decree already mentioned in Acts. Here the spirit is one of compromise with the Judaizers. The very fact that it was necessary to issue such a decree suggests that Jesus had never spoken on this subject or the apostles could have appealed to his words.

Exception for Unchastity.—The primary passages suggesting that marriage is dissoluble for unchastity are two from Matthew's Gospel.

> And the Pharisees came up to him and tested him by asking, "Is it lawful to divorce one's wife for any cause?" He answered, "Have you not read that he who made them from the beginning made them male

> and female, and said, 'For this reason a man shall leave his father and mother and be joined to his wife, and the two shall become one?' So they are no longer two but one. What therefore God has joined together, let no man put asunder." They said to him, "Why then did Moses command one to give a certificate of divorce, and to put her away?" He said to them, "For your hardness of heart Moses allowed you to divorce your wives, but from the beginning it was not so. And I say to you: whoever divorces his wife except for unchastity, and marries another, commits adultery."[122]
>
> It was also said, "Whoever divorces his wife, let him give her a certificate of divorce." But I say to you that everyone who divorces his wife, except on the ground of unchastity, makes her an adulteress; and whoever marries a divorced woman commits adultery.[123]

The fundamental complaint against the "exception" passages is that they are seemingly in contradiction to what Jesus said about divorce in Mark and its parallel in Luke and with Paul's teaching in First Corinthians. In these passages there is no suggestion of the possibility of divorce. Several suggestions have been made toward a solution of this problem.

It is not impossible for Jesus to have assumed the exception clause in the non-Matthean passages. Jesus on occasion used language that was absolute, but did not necessarily mean it to be that way. An example of such hyperbole are his instructions about oaths: "But I say to you, swear not at all."[124] This passage, like Matthew 5:32, occurs in the Sermon on the Mount where Jesus had just contrasted the use of oaths under the Old Covenant. Normative Christianity has never taken this as absolute, nor did Jesus who virtually allowed himself to be put on his oath by the high priest.[125] It has been suggested that Jesus was able to take the exception for unchastity for granted because unchastity automatically dissolved the union.[126] There is some evidence that the Jews, after the disappearance of the death penalty for adultery, made divorce in the case of adultery mandatory.[127] The most drastic solution, however, is that of R. H. Charles who rejects the historical character of the Markan passage.[128] If it is granted that the Matthean passages represent an exception to the indissolubility of marriage, then there are three common interpretations of their meaning.

Unchastity.—The crucial word in the text is πορνεία which the Revised Standard Version translates "unchastity." Its occurrence in the LXX and the New Testament would indicate a wider meaning than the King James translation of "fornication." In the Old Testament πορνεία is used in connection with the widow Tamar.[129] That it is applicable even to married women is indicated in the story of Gomer, Hosea's wife. [130] In the new Testament it is found twenty-two times with a wide variety of meanings. Frequently it refers to illicit sexual intercourse in general,[131] and can even be used to describe an incestuous relationship.[132] While πορνεία can include adulterous unions, it is a broader term than either "adultery" or "fornication." Although illicit sexual connections involving married individuals would most often mean "adultery," it should not be overlooked that a more appropriate term would be "unchastity" which is as broad as πορνεία itself.

Typical Exception.—According to this view, first reflected in Origen,[133] the exception clause is taken as a typical ground for divorce and not as the only ground on which a union can be dissolved.[134] To make unchastity representative of other sexual vices, is to rob the Matthean passages of all precision of language. If a precept is given and an exception stated in specific language, it is difficult to maintain the meaning of language and at the same time view the sole exception as typical of many exceptions. What would prompt Jesus to reply in this vein? It is certainly not apparent why one would say that divorce was permitted only for one reason, if the reason is so inclusive as to cover sexual sins in general.

Spiritual Adultery.—Another interpretation of πορνεία commonly offered is that it refers not only to the physical act of adultery, but also to spiritual adultery. This view apparently was first suggested by Augustine. In his book *Adulterous Marriages*, in a context pertaining to mixed marriages, he states, "Because of any kind of fornication —whether it be of the flesh or spirit, wherein also understood—it is not lawful for a wife to marry after a husband has been put away . . ."[135] By this means, the Bishop of

Hippo is able to reconcile Jesus' exception and the Pauline Privilege,[136] which says a believer is not bound if a non-believing mate departs. Participation in a false religion, so Augustine reasoned, was spiritual adultery. It must be possible, therefore, to divorce one who persists in spiritual adultery. The application of the term "adultery" for apostasy is a familiar one in the Old Testament,[137] and its use pertaining to Christianity would be a natural projection, as is indicated by the New Testament.[138] While it is possible to spiritualize the idea of adultery, it seems impossible to spiritualize the context of the Matthean passages to make this solution appropriate.

The Pauline Privilege.—The most important passage relating to the New Testament doctrine of divorce, outside the Gospels, is what is frequently referred to as "The Pauline Privilege." In First Corinthians Paul, having spoken of certain evils in the church, passes on to answer specific questions which had been put to him by the Grecian Church. These are easily identifiable by the recurring phrase, "now concerning," with which he begins each section. It is in the seventh chapter that the first of these replies is found, and the first deals with problems related to marriage.

> Now concerning the matters about which you wrote. It is well for a man not to touch a woman. But because of the temptation to immorality, each man should have his own wife and each woman her own husband.[139]

Paul continues to discuss three situations in Corinth.

> To the unmarried and the widows I say that it is well for them to remain single as I do. But if they cannot exercise self control, they should marry. For it is better to marry than to be aflame with passion.[140]
>
> To the married I give charge, not I but the Lord, that the wife should not separate from her husband (but if she does, let her remain single or else be reconciled to her husband)—and that the husband should not divorce his wife.[141]
>
> To the rest I say, not the Lord, that if any brother has a wife who is an unbeliever, and she consents to live with him, he should not divorce her. If any woman has a husband who is an unbeliever, and he consents to live with her, she should not divorce him. For the unbelieving husband is consecrated through his wife, and the unbelieving wife is consecrated through her husband. Otherwise, your children would be unclean, but as it is they are holy. But if the unbelieving partner desires to separate, let it be so; in such a case the brother or sister is not bound. For God has called us to peace. Wife, how do you know whether you will save your husband? Husband how do you know whether you will save your wife?[142]

These three excerpts from the chapter show the comprehensive character of the apostle's instructions. Each section began with a formula which included the words "I say" or "command," and the three categories are named as "the unmarried and the widows," "the married," and "the rest." Since under the heading of the "married" Paul discusses situations where both parties were Christians, the only category for "the rest" is that of mixed marriages. It is not without significance that Paul gives such unions separate consideration. It is only in regard to the "married" group that Paul claims to have a word of the Lord. Concerning the single and pagan-Christian marriages he gives his own judgment.

The Matter of Authority.—It is essential to a correct understanding of the problem to realize that when Paul distinguishes between what the Lord says and what he says, he does not mean to imply that his words are merely good advice to be taken at the discretion of the readers. While it is true that he only uses the word "command" when he has a word of the Lord, reserving "speak" for his own utterances, his instructions are given on the basis of his apostolic authority. As Robertson and Plummer have pointed out, Paul is not distinguishing between inspired and uninspired utterances of his own, but between what the Lord said and what the apostle said.[143] Paul had no precept from Jesus in the case of the unmarried and in the case of marriages involving pagans and Christians. Paul speaks as an apostle, who, as he reminds the readers in Corinth in the closing verse of the chapter, possesses the Holy Spirit.[144]

The Corinthian Problem.—It must be remembered that Paul, in discussing mixed marriages between Christians and pagans is doing so in reply to a specific question he had received from them. The question is one of possible contamination of the Christian by the non-Christian. This is clear from the passage itself.

> For the unbelieving husband is consecrated through his wife, and the unbelieving wife is consecrated through her husband. Otherwise, your children would be unclean, but as it is they are holy.[145]

This matter of uncleanliness would be a problem for a partially Jewish community. Mixed marriages were frowned on from post-exilic times, although they were frequently formed.[146] In Judaism if a mate was converted from the faith, it was sufficient grounds for divorce.[147] Social relations between a Jew and a non-Jew would, on the analogy of Haggai 2:11-13, render one ceremonially unclean. Apparently there were enough Jewish Christians in Corinth, or enough who were familiar with the teachings of Judaism, to make the mixed marriages of Christians a problem. Paul's reply is that instead of uncleanliness being communicated, consecration is passed from the Christian to the unbelieving partner. It is for this reason that children born to such a union are holy. This makes it clear, as Charles suggests,[148] that the breach of the union of the mixed married was not due to adultery or any similar reason.

Separation.—It is not certain that divorce is sanctioned in this paragraph. This can be seen by observing that the text says "should not divorce" in verses 13 and 14 and by the fact that where permission is granted it merely says "separate" and that the Christian "is not bound." This question can only be decided by a consideration of the

Greek text. On both occasions where the Revised Standard Version translates "divorce," it is ἀφιέναι, while the permission is called "separation" and is a translation of χωρισθῆναι. There are four possible meanings which this passage can have: (1) both verbs mean to "divorce"; (2) both words mean "to depart" in the sense of the English word "separate"; (3) χωρισθῆναι means "to divorce" while ἀφιέναι means "to depart"; (4) χωρισθῆναι means to "depart" and ἀφιέναι means "to divorce." The correct meaning can be ascertained at the previous place in the chapter where both words occur.[149] In discussing the marriage of Christians, Paul says that a wife should not be separated (χωρισθῆναι) and if separated (χωρισθῆναι) she should not remarry. The husband, he further says, should not divorce (ἀφιέναι) his wife. Here both words are used as synonyms for divorce. The reason Paul used ἀφιέναι is not that he means anything different than χωρισθῆναι, but he reflects a Jewish background in which a wife could depart from her husband, but only the husband had the prerogative of divorcing (sending away) the wife.[150] That this is the case is also seen from the fact that the definition of χωρισθῆναι must have been large enough to permit the possibility of remarriage or else Paul would not have felt the necessity of counselling against it.

Remarriage.—Naturally, if there was disagreement over whether the Pauline Privilege permitted divorce, there would also be a lack of unanimity concerning the right to remarry. It has been shown that there is surely the right to divorce. Three views are held concerning the right to remarry: (1) some deny that the passage gives the right to remarry;[151] (2) others are extremely cautious about remarriage;[152] and (3) others affirm the right to remarry as being explicit in the passage.[153] The key verse is the fifteenth:

> But if the unbelieving partner desires to separate, let it be so; in such a case the brother or sister is not bound. For God has called us to peace.

Keeping in mind what has been said about the synonymity of χωρισθῆναι and ἀφιέναι it is difficult to imagine these words being used and not meaning the right of remarriage. In the previous paragraph in the same chapter, Paul used χωρισθῆναι and then carefully qualified it so as to show that he did not mean for it to be understood in its usual sense of permitting remarriage. In the passage under consideration, no such qualification is given. If the unbeliever desires to separate (divorce), let him go. Paul says the Christian is not bound. According to the Mishnah, the most important phrase in a Jewish divorce bill was, "you are free to any man."[154] The meaning of "bound" (δεδούλωται) is, of course, crucial to the interpretation which says that remarriage is permitted. To what is the person not bound? Some say Paul simply means that the Christian is not under obligation to keep the partner in the home.[155] This seems rather a strange obligation for the Christian to have if the partner is already departed. Others say it means the Christian is not bound to the marriage and is free to remarry.[156]

"Bound" is from δεδούλωται which has the lexical form of δουλόω. In verse 39, Paul also uses the idea of bondage and applies it to marriage: "A wife is bound to her husband as long as he lives. If the husband dies, she is free to be married to whom she wishes, only in the Lord." It is true that the "bound" in this verse is δέδεται which has the lexical form of δέω. While two different words are used for the bondage he discusses in verse 39, they are ultimately related to a common root, δοῦλος. The idea of bondage is also applied to marriage in verse 27 where Paul exhorts, "Are you bound to a wife? Do not seek to be free." Again he uses δέδεται, a form of δέω. He also uses "bound" in Romans 7:2 in reference to marriage. One explanation of the fact that the Pauline Privilege is denied is that there was a hesitancy to admit another cause for divorce than the one mentioned in the Synoptic Gospels. But Paul said that what he wrote concerning the mixed marriage was on his own authority rather than being a command of the Lord. Jesus, by the very nature of his ministry, would not have spoken to a situation involving a Jew and a pagan, since he deemed his mission to be to the House of Israel.

Summary.—From the foregoing discussion, it seems possible to draw the following conclusions: (1) Paul permits Christians who are partners in a mixed marriage to be divorced if the non-believer so desires; (2) the Christian is therefore not under bondage and is free to remarry; (3) Paul is stating on his apostolic authority a reason for divorce not previously mentioned in the New Testament.

Attitude Toward Candidates for Baptism

The New Testament does not address itself specifically to the situation of those divorced and remarried before conversion. The closest event in the ministry of Jesus to the matter of multiple marriage is the Samaritan woman. She had been married to five men and was currently living with a lover.[157] While the text only states that many of the Samaritans believed because of her witness to Christ, the implication is that she was also a disciple of Jesus. It does not say, unfortunately, what moral reforms the woman was required to make. It is significant, however, that Jesus distinguished between husbands and lovers. If he did not accept the validity of remarriage and divorce, then the woman would have had only one husband and several lovers. In the qualifications for elders and widows, the Pastoral Epistles may provide evidence for the Church's view on this matter. Although it is not certain that "one-woman man"[158] and "one-man woman"[159] refer to individuals who have not been divorced or to those who have not remarried after the death of a mate, it is a possibility that it refers to the former. If this is the case, then there were divorced individuals in the Church. Perhaps the most significant, however, of all the New Testament passages is that of the Pauline Privilege. Paul clearly makes a distinction between couples who are Christians and those who belong to a mixed marriage as far as the indissolubility of their respective marriages is concerned. He makes a distinction between the marital ethics of saints and sinners.[160] This is also seen in Paul's remark that it is not the church's responsibility to judge the outsider.[161]

Since divorce was a common practice in both Jewish and Roman society, it is inconceivable that the church of the New Testament period was never confronted by a divorced and remarried believer who wished to respond to the Gospel. The silence of the New Testament on the matter can either be explained as accidental or an indication that the Church was unconcerned about the marital status of a baptismal candidate. The latter is suggested by Paul who reminds them, in a context dealing with marital problems, that:

> . . . God has called us to peace . . . Only, let every one lead the life which the Lord has assigned to him, and in which God has called him. This is my rule in all the churches ... Every one should remain in the state in which he was called ... So brethren in whatever state each was called, there let him remain with God.[162]

Although pagans were not responsible for Christian ethics, they were not free from moral guidance or responsibility. Their situation was similar to that of the Gentiles in relation to Judaism. The Jews viewed the pagans as being in a covenant that God made with Noah.[163] The obligations of this covenant are listed by the rabbis as: prohibition of worship of other gods; prohibition of blasphemy; establishment of courts of justice; prohibition of murder; prohibition of adultery; prohibition of robbery;

and prohibition of eating flesh containing blood.[164] These items are called the Noahic Laws. The Gentile covenant is mentioned by Isaiah: "The earth lies polluted under its inhabitants; for they have transgressed the laws, violated the statutes, broken the everlasting covenant."[165] Jesus uses the covenant motif in the Last Supper as an explanation for his death.[166] It occurs also outside the Gospels.[167] Christianity is both the fulfillment of Abraham's covenant and the beginning of a new one. Those who have been baptized into Christ, Paul states, are heirs of the covenantal promise.[168] It follows that those who are outside the Church are not a part of the New Covenant.[169] The Noahic covenant idea is suggested by the Apostolic Decree in Acts 15. Instead of being obligated for the entire Jewish Law, Gentile Christians were told to abstain from idolatry, fornication, from what is strangled, and from blood.[170] This list is similar to the Noahic Laws and may suggest that the Apostolic Decree proscribed this as a minimum requirement for Gentile Christians. The basis for Gentile morals is also that of natural revelation. This is presented by Paul in his description of the condition of the Gentile world in the opening chapters of Romans. He reminds them that God's wrath is being revealed to them because they had an adequate revelation of God's essential qualities from nature.[171] In the second chapter, the situation is spelled out in greater detail.

> When Gentiles who have not the law do by nature what the law requires, they are a law to themselves, even though they do not have the law. They show

> that what the law required is written on their hearts, while their conscience also bears witness and their conflicting thoughts accuse or perhaps excuse them on that day when, according to my Gospel, God judges the secrets of men by Christ Jesus.[172]

That this idea of natural revelation is employed by Paul in his approach to Gentiles is indicated by his Areopagus Speech.[173] The development of his message to the Athenians is: God is creator and sustainer of the world; the knowledge of God in nature is such that all should seek him, but the Athenians have not and consequently ended in idolatry; while in the past God has not intervened, he now commands men to repent in preparation for the judgment by Christ. The affinity of this with Romans is apparent. And it is to this idea that Paul appeals when he says nature teaches about the length of men's hair.[174]

Adultery is prohibited by both the rabbinic idea of the covenant with Noah and by Paul's concept of the inward law. In listing the vices for which Gentiles are condemned, the Apostle specifies adultery.[175] This means that Gentiles are held accountable for adulterous relations; but it must be remembered that "adultery" in neither of these circumstances is defined by Christianity. In Christianity, adultery includes all extra-marital relations in a monogamous union. In Judaism adultery was differently defined because polygamy was sanctioned and divorce and remarriage accepted. A person could have a plurality of wives or a succession of wives and neither would be adulterous in nature. Since the basis on which the responsibility of the

Gentiles is defined is that of natural revelation, which did not include Christian marital ethics, then the silence of the New Testament concerning the marital status of converts is not accidental but by design.

SEX MORALITY

The sex morality reflected in the New Testament is in one sense merely an extension of the subjects as discussed in the chapters pertaining to Judaism and Hellenism. It is an added witness to the conditions in those cultural situations as well as a clear indication of what the Christian message encountered.

Premarital Sex Morals

Jesus makes it clear that his followers must not only abstain from the overt acts of fornication and licentiousness,[176] but the evil intention as well.[177] Their conduct in sexual matters is related to the final judgment.[178] Jesus showed a great sympathy toward offenders. He ranked harlots before the Pharisees,[179] not because he considered their actions of no consequence, but because they, knowing their sinful condition, were closer to repentance than the Pharisees who deemed themselves righteous. Jesus, according to the accounts of the Gospels, does not refer directly to homosexuality, although the word πορνεία is broad enough to include the practice. More likely, he found no need to speak directly against it since the Jews were highly critical of it, and it was probably rare in Palestine.

It is to pass from one world to another to turn from Jesus' instructions to those of Paul. Whereas Jesus taught against a Jewish background with its high moral fiber, Paul moved with the Gospel into the Gentile world. All of Paul's epistles reflect the difficulty he had with Gentile converts who were not entirely free from their Gentile sex practices.

Fornication.—In Paul's list of vices, the word "fornication" receives special attention. Usually it is listed first and in some places is mentioned more than once.[180] It also occurs in the Pastoral Epistles,[181] and also in Hebrews,[182] and in the book of Revelation.[183] In the books where πορνεία is not found, frequently some synonym, such as "lusts," ἐπιθυμίαι, conveys the same thought.[184]

Prostitution.—Comparatively little is said specifically about prostitution in the Epistles, perhaps because it was comprehended in more general terms. The most detailed discussion occurs in Paul's Corinthian correspondence, significantly enough to a church in a city especially noted for prostitution.

> Do you know that he who joins himself to a prostitute becomes one body with her? For, as it is written, "The two shall become one."[185]

Paul warns that to attach oneself to a prostitute is to detach oneself from Christ. It has been suggested that the harlot was a priestess of Aphrodite and that whereas sexual union with the cult prostitutes supposedly brought consecration, Paul warns that it really brings desecration.[186] It is this cult relationship, and not strictly the commercial vice, which results in such a bold statement by the Apostle.[187] Harlotry is especially singled out in the Apocalypse for attention. The figure of the great harlot is introduced as the supremely evil figure.[188] She is said to have "corrupted the earth with her fornication." And harlots are said to receive their final abode in "the lake that burns with fire.[189]

Incest.—What is probably a case of incest is reported by Paul in Corinthians when he discusses the man who has "his father's wife."[190] This situation is especially painful to Paul because such hardened immorality is not practiced extensively by pagans.

Homosexuality.—The Epistles are comparatively silent on the subject of homosexuality, considering its prevalency in the ancient world. The subject receives its fullest treatment in Romans. In the first chapter Paul, having suggested that the Gentiles had some knowledge of God from the creation, says that they chose to ignore him. This resulted in idolatry, which in turn resulted in sexual abuse. Paul describes the situation in the following words:

> For this reason God gave them up to dishonorable passions. Their women exchanged natural relations for unnatural, and the men likewise gave up natural relations with women and were consumed with passions for one another, men committing shameless acts with men and receiving in their own persons the

due penalty for their error.[191]

Homosexuality has a double appearance in the list of vices in I Corinthians where "effeminate" μαλακοί and "abusers with men" ἀρσενοκοῖται are both listed, although the Revised Standard Version joins the two Greek words together by a simple rendering of "homosexuals."[192] The latter word also occurs in the Pastoral Epistles.[193] Also under this heading should be considered the use of ἀσέλγεια which is rendered "unnatural lust."[194]

Postmarital Sexual Morals

Since it has already been indicated above that the word "fornication" was a general enough term to include all unchastity, there is no need to repeat what has been said by Jesus and already discussed under the heading of premarital morals. It is significant that Jesus, by envisioning a woman divorcing her husband, thereby denied the double ethical standard and the sexual freedom permitted man in Jewish thought.[195] Adulteries (μοικεῖαι) occur on Jesus' list of vices in the Gospels.[196] It was a sin so serious, if the Matthean passages are accepted as authentic, that it provided sufficient grounds to dissolve an otherwise indissoluble marriage. Adultery does not frequently appear on Paul's vice-lists.[197] He has, in fact, little to say about the act. One reason for this is that he reserved the word μοιχεία for the illicit sexual relations of a married woman.[198] In so doing he was being true to his Jewish background, although he certainly believed a husband could sin against his marriage. Specifically, he speaks of a woman becoming an adulteress if she marries while her husband is alive;[199] twice he quotes the Seventh Commandment;[200] and once distinguished between fornicators and adulterers.[201] Apparently, he includes the act of adultery in such words as πορνεία. Paul is certainly concerned about sexual impurity and obviously judged this to be one of his greatest problems. In many places in the world of his day religious expressions and sexual expressions were closely linked. Immorality had, if not the blessing, at least the toleration of many mystery religions. It also thrived under a general indifference as to its seriousness. Even in the Church there were those who still reflected this idea that sex, like other appetites, should be freely satisfied. Against this, Paul fought vehemently. His solution was varied: avoid contact with immoral people[202] or find satisfaction through marriage.[203] When these failed, a last remedial step for the Church was to deny fellowship to immoral Christians.[204]

CONCLUSIONS

The New Testament reflects its Jewish heritage in the high regard in which it holds marriage. Jesus used the marital union in many of his Kingdom parables, and Paul employed it to describe the relationship between Christ and the Church. Although marriage is highly esteemed, there is no specific statement concerning the form, while from general passages it is clear that it is monogamous.

There were forces at work in Christianity, as in Judaism, which tended to disparage matrimony. This was not, however, from a spirit of asceticism, but from the conviction that marriage, like all human loyalties, should be subordinate to the Kingdom of God. In Paul this found expression in the greater freedom the celibate would have in accomplishing the Lord's work. The New Testament shows more of the Roman than the Jewish spirit in its attitude toward digamy. Although second marriages were not prohibited, they were regulated and discouraged.

Divorce was an institution in both Roman and Jewish societies and it is not surprising that the New Testament has much to say on the subject. In Mark, Luke, and Paul, no grounds for divorce are mentioned, which would suggest that marriage is indissoluble. This conclusion, however, is difficult since Matthew twice mentions that divorce is possible for unchastity. Several solutions to this seeming contradiction have been offered.

Frequently it is maintained that all that is meant by divorce in the Matthean passages is separation from bed and board. This requires that the word ἀπολύειν have two quite different meanings in the same context. Also against such a view is the fact that separation as an accepted terminal solution to marriage was not practiced among the Jews.

Another possible solution is that the exception clauses did not originally belong to the text. There is some textual evidence in support of this position, the Vaticanus being the chief witness. The texts supporting "B" in the variant reading, however, are more numerous for the last half of the phrase, ποιεῖ αὐτὴν μοιχευθῆναι, than for the crucial words, παρεκτὸς λόγου. The critical editors of the Greek text have unanimously supported the accepted reading.

Closely related to the above is a frequently expressed Protestant view that the exception clause is an interpolation. This is a conclusion reached without textual support and is further made precarious by the fact that the vast majority of the Fathers show evidence of knowing Matthew with the exception clauses.

The indissolubility of marriage is maintained by others through the interpretation that πορνεία refers to premarital unchastity. This is based on the Old Testament law concerning virgins. This view would be unintelligible in the context in Matthew 5:32. It also has against it the fact that the Church Fathers show no familiarity with it.

Others admit that the clause represents a genuine exception to the indissolubility of marriage, but maintain that this was only a temporary concession which Jesus granted the Jews. This position, likewise, would be unintelligible in the context of Matthew 5:32 where Jesus contrasted the Mosaic Law with the new ethics he taught.

The exception clause, other scholars say, represents not an exception to the verb, but to the entire sentence. The result would be that Jesus passed over the matter of unchastity rather than focusing attention on it. While this is a possible explanation, it is difficult to understand why Jesus brought up the subject just to dismiss it. Also, the other preteritive passages in the New Testament are not comparable to this verse in construction.

The interpretation that is called the "corrective" view sees Jesus as correctly interpreting the Mosaic Law for the Jews who had misunderstood it as permitting divorce. Jesus' reply, therefore, would be merely academic as far as Christians are concerned. This is possible in Matthew 19:9, but it is quite impossible in 5:32 where Jesus is contrasting what he says with what Moses has said.

The "inclusive" interpretation would make Jesus say there is no ground for divorce, not even the case of unchastity. This view depends upon questionable grammatical assumptions involving μὴ ἐπὶ πορνείᾳ in Matthew 19:9. Even if these were granted, the view is rendered inadequate by the fact that Matthew 5:32 uses a different statement (παρεκτὸς λόγου πορνείας) for the exception clause. Had Jesus wanted to include unchastity among the inadequate reasons for divorce, he could have done so by merely adding one word, καί.

A solution to this problem which has gained support among Catholic scholars is that which sees πορνεία as a reference to an illegal wife. Such unions were viewed as null and void in the Old Testament. It is based on the use of *zona*, "prostitute," in post-biblical literature for illegal wives. Esau, who married an illegal wife, that is, a "stranger," is said to be a fornicator (πόρνος) in the New Testament. Likewise, the incestuous relationship in the Church in Corinth is called πορνεία. And the Gentile Christians are told to abstain from πορνεία in the Apostolic Decree in Acts. The basis for the Decree was an attempt to compromise with the Jewish Christians who thought it necessary for the Gentile converts to keep the Law. The prohibition of πορνεία must refer to marriages within the prohibited degrees of Leviticus 18. It is concluded on the basis of these references that in the New Testament πορνεία can refer to illegal or *zenout* marriages. While this is a clever solution, it is strange that Jesus would introduce into Matthew 19:9 a matter about which there was no disagreement with the Jews. Why would he say that *zenout* marriages were invalid? That he did not say this is actually indicated by the Apostolic Decree. If Jesus had spoken on this subject, it would hardly have been necessary for the apostles to have had the conference in Jerusalem. That they did not appeal to his words is probably an indication that this was not what Jesus meant by the exception clause.

None of the solutions to the apparent contradiction of the exception clauses with other passages in the New Testament is without serious problems which render their acceptance difficult or impossible. The search for some harmony is, in fact, based on two presuppositions. The first is that there can be no contradictions in what Jesus is reported to have said. The second is that Jesus' words in Mark and Luke represent absolute statements. If either of these assumptions is abandoned, it is possible to take the Matthean passages in their most logical and apparent meaning, that is, divorce is permissible for πορνεία. The meaning of πορνεία should not be limited to "fornication" or "adultery" but is best translated by "unchastity."

Indicative that marriage was not viewed as absolutely indissoluble in every case is the Pauline Privilege of First Corinthians. Although a Christian couple is not to divorce, it is possible for a Christian who is joined to a pagan to be divorced, if the pagan desires the break. Attempts to view this permission as only the granting of the right of separation fails on two accounts. First, the words "divorce" (ἀφιέναι) and "separate" (χωρισθῆναι) both mean divorce. Second, Paul employs them, not in a way to indicate a difference between them, but in the light of his Jewish background that a wife's action is a "departing" while only the husband has the prerogative of "divorcing."

Divorce in both Jewish and Roman societies carried with it the right to remarry. On the one occasion in the Pauline writings in which remarriage is specifically denied, Paul uses "divorce" (χωρισθῆναι), and then immediately qualifies it to indicate he does not mean the normal divorce with the right to remarry, but only a temporary separation. In the exemption clause in Matthew, there is no specific statement as to the right of the innocent party to remarry, although 19:9 says, "Whoever divorces his wife, except for unchastity, and marries another, commits adultery." This implies the right of remarriage for a person who divorces his adulterous mate. The guilty party is specifically denied the right to remarry.

There is no direct evidence in the New Testament to

indicate the attitude of the Apostolic Church toward a divorced and remarried catechumen. Since there was considerable freedom to divorce in both Roman and Jewish society, it is likely that the expanding church had to face the problem. The silence of the New Testament can either be accidental or indicative that pre-Christian morality was unimportant. The circumstantial evidence would indicate the latter. As the Jews did not hold the pagans responsible for observing the Law of Moses, so Christians did not hold pagans accountable for Christian ethics. In both Judaism and Christianity the distinction is made on the basis of the covenant. This is not to suggest that the pagan was without moral guidance or responsibility. The basis for his conduct was natural revelation. This is indicated by Paul in his description of the Gentile situation, by his approach to Gentile preaching, and an appeal to common ideals held by both pagans and Christians.

Jesus desired that his followers abstain not only from the immoral act, but from the immoral desire as well. He indicated, however, a sympathy for those who had fallen into sexual sins. Jesus does not speak directly to the problem of homosexuality, probably because it was not a widespread practice in Judaism. When Christianity moved into the Gentile world, a change took place in its approach to morality. Paul was required to deal frequently with the problem of sex morality. Unchastity (πορνεία) is included in Paul's vice-lists and usually is first in order. Paul has little to say directly about adultery, incest, or homosexuality, although what he does say about the latter reflects a great abhorrence. Paul was required to give his attention to sexual morality because of the background from which the converts came. On one occasion he speaks of fornicators, adulterers, and homosexuals, and adds, "as such were some of you."[205] Some apparently continued immoral conduct after their conversions, and this should not be unexpected. "They have been declared to be in right relations with God, not that they had been of right moral character or had been made of such."[206] The entire stress of moral instruction was to bring their characters into accordance with that relationship.

Chapter IV Footnotes

[1]Jn. 2:1-11.
[2]Matt. 5:27-32.
[3]Matt. 8:11.
[4]Matt. 22:2.
[5]Mk. 2:19-20.
[6]Jn. 3:29.
[7]Matt. 19:4.
[8]Matt. 19:10.
[9]I Cor. 7:39.
[10]I Thess. 4:4.
[11]II Cor. 11:2.
[12]*Supra*, p. 51.
[13]Otto Piper, *The Christian Interpretation of Sex* (New York: Charles Scribner's Sons, 1953), p. 82 f.
[14]I Tim. 4:4.
[15]Heb. 13:4.
[16]Acts 5:1; 18:26; Rom. 16:3; I Cor. 9:5; 14:35; Col. 3:18 f.; I Tim. 3:2.
[17]*Supra*, p. 62.
[18]Matt. 19:5.
[19]David Daube, *op. cit.*, p. 81.
[20]*Ibid.*
[21]I Cor. 7:2.
[22]Eph. 5:23.
[23]I Tim. 3:2.
[24]I Tim. 5:9.
[25]*Supra*, pp. 26, 30.
[26]Matt. 19:12.
[27]Lk. 14:20; 17:26-30.
[28]H. L. Strack and Paul Billerbeck, *Kommentar zum Neuen Testament aus Talmud und Midrasch* (München: C. H. Beck, 1922), Vol. I, p. 805 f.
[29]H. D. A. Major, T. W. Manson, and C. J. Wright, *The Mission and Message of Jesus* (New York: R. P. Dutton, 1938), p. 507.
[30]*Educator*, iii. 4.26.
[31]Rudolf Bultmann, *Jesus and the Word* (New York: Charles

Scribner's Sons, 1934), p. 101.

[32]Matt. 19:11.

[33]II Cor. 11:2; Eph. 5:23.

[34]M. R. James, *The Apocryphal New Testament* (Oxford: Clarendon Press, 1924), p. 10 f.

[35]I Cor. 7:1.

[36]Gen. 20:6; Prov. 6:29.

[37]C. H. Dodd, *Gospel and Law* (New York: Columbia University Press, 1951), pp. 25-28; John C. Cooper, "St. Paul's Evaluation of Women and Marriage," *Lutheran Quarterly*, XVI (Gettysburg, 1964), pp. 291-302.

[38]I Cor. 7:36-38.

[39]Fernand Prat, *The Theology of Saint Paul* (London: Burns Oates and Washbourne, 1945), p. 105; G. Findley, *Expositor's Greek Testament* (London: Hodder and Stoughton, 1900), Vol. II, p. 836; F. W. Grosheide, *Commentary on the First Epistle to the Corinthians* (Grand Rapids: Wm. B. Eerdmans, 1953), p. 182; A. Robertson and A. Plummer, *First Epistle of Saint Paul to the Corinthians* in *The International Critical Commentary* (New York: Charles Scribner's Sons, 1911), p. 158 f.

[40]William Arndt and Wilbur Gingrich, *A Greek-English Lexicon of the New Testament and Other Early Christian Literature* (Chicago: The University of Chicago Press, 1957), p. 150.

[41]Clarence T. Craig, *The Interpreter's Bible, The First Epistle to the Corinthians* (New York: Abingdon-Cokesbury Press, 1953), p. 87; H. Achelis, "Agapetae," *Encyclopaedia of Religion and Ethics*, ed. James Hasting (New York: Charles Scribner's Sons, 1928), Vol. I, p. 179.

[42]James Moffatt, *The First Epistle of Paul to the Corinthians* (London: Hodder and Stoughton, 1938), p. 67.

[43]Acts 21:9.

[44]Rev. 19:7, 9; 21:2, 9 f; 22:17.

[45]*Supra*, p. 58.

[46]Rom. 7:2-3.

[47]I Cor. 7:39-40.

[48]*Supra*, p. 71.

[49]I Cor. 7:8, 27, 40.

[50]I Cor. 7:39.

[51]Adolf Harnack, *op. cit.*, I, 81; Tertullian, *To His Wife*, ii. 1-2.

[52]I Tim. 5:11.

[53]E. K. Simpson, *The Pastoral Epistles* (Grand Rapids: Wm. B. Eerdmans, 1954), p. 50.

[54]Walter Lock, *The Pastoral Epistles*, in the *International Critical Commentary* (Edinburgh: T. and T. Clark, 1924), p. 36.

[55]Burton Scott Easton, *The Pastoral Epistles* (New York: Charles Scribner's Sons, 1947), p. 212.

[56]P. C. Spicq, *Les Épitres Pastorales* (Paris: Librairie Lecoffre, 1947), p. 78.

[57]O. D. Watkins, *Holy Matrimony* (London: Rivington, Percival and Company, 1895), p. 593.

[58]J. B. Frey, "La signification des termes *monandros* et *univira*," *Recherches de science religieuse*, XX (1930), 57.

[59]*Supra*, pp. 54-56.

[60]I Cor. 7:10-11.

[61]I Cor. 7:39.

[62]Rom. 7:1-3.

[63]Charles Gore, *The Question of Divorce* (New York: Charles Scribner's Sons, 1911), p. 23; T. A. Lacey, *Marriage in Church and State* (London: Robert Scott, 1912), p. 22; Felix L. Cirlot, *Christ and Divorce* (Lexington, Ky.: Trafton Publishing Company, 1945), p. 37; Francis Gigot, *Christ's Teaching Concerning Divorce in the New Testament* (New York: Benziger Brothers, 1912), p. 63; J. J. von Allmen, *Marie et femmes d'après Saint Paul* (Paris: Delachaux and Niestle, 1951), p. 41.

[64]Matt. 5:32.

[65]Matt. 19:9.

[66]Fernand Prat, *Jesus Christ; His Life, His Teaching, and His Work* (Milwaukee: Bruce Publishing Company, 1950), Vol. II, p. 81; Joseph Bonsirven, *Les enseignements de Jesus-Christ* (Paris: Besuchesne et ses fils, 1950), p. 203.

[67]Bruce Vawter, "The Divorce Clause in Mt. 5:32 and 19:9," *The Catholic Biblical Quarterly* (1954), XVI, p. 152.

[68]O. D. Watkins, *Holy Matrimony, op. cit.*, p. 152.

[69]G. H. Joyce, *op. cit.*, p. 283.

[70]Burton Scott Easton, "Divorce in the New Testament,"

Anglican Theological Review, XXII (April, 1940), p. 114.

[71]R. H. Charles, *The Teaching of the New Testament on Divorce* (London: Williams and Norgate, 1921), pp. 27-31.

[72]*Commentary on Saint Matthew,* xix.

[73]*Stromata,* ii. 23.

[74]*Ibid.,* iii.

[75]Cirlot, *op. cit.,* p. 10.

[76]*Against Marcion,* iv. 34.

[77]O. D. Watkins, *Holy Matrimony, op. cit.,* p. 171.

[78]Sherman E. Johnson, *The Interpreter's Bible, The Gospel According to Saint Matthew* (New York: Abingdon-Cokesbury, 1951), VII, 299.

[79]Willoughby C. Allen, *A Critical and Exegetical Commentary on the Gospel According to Saint Matthew* (New York: Charles Scribner's Sons, 1907), p. 204; Alfred Plummer, *An Exegetical Commentary on the Gospel According to Saint Matthew* (London: Scott, 1928), p. 259 f.; Kirsopp Lake, "The Earliest Christian Teaching on Divorce," *Expositor,* 7th Series, X (1910), 422.

[80]Sherman E. Johnson, *op. cit.,* p. 299.

[81]Willoughby Allen, *op. cit.,* p. 52.

[82]*Supra,* p. 107 f.

[83]M. J. Lagrange, *Évangile selon saint Matthieu* (Paris: J. Gabalda et Fils, 1927), pp. 366-370; Alfred Edersheim, *The Life and Times of Jesus the Messiah* (New York: Longmans, 1910), II, 335; B. Weiss, *Die vier Evangelien* (Leipzig: J. C. Hinrich, 1903), pp. 118, 336; Joseph Bonsirven, *Le Divorce dans le Nouveau Testament* (Paris: Desceles et Cie, 1948), p. 41; R. Souarn, "Adultère," *Dictionaire de Théologie Catholique (Paris:* Librairie Letousey et Ané, 1939), I, pt. 1, p. 471.

[84]F. H. Chase, *What Did Christ Teach About Divorce?* (London: S.P.C.K., 1921), p. 28; J. von Döllinger, *First Ages of the Church* (London: Gibbings and Company, 1866), II, 310.

[85]Deut. 22:20-21.

[86]Amos 7:17; Ecclus. 26. 12.

[87]R. Souarn, *op. cit.,* p. 471.

[88]Fernand Prat, *Jesus Christ, op. cit.,* p. 81; Joseph Bonsirven, *Le Divorce, op. cit.,* p. 38 f; R. Souarn, *op. cit.,* p. 471; G. H. Joyce, *Christian Marriage* (London: Sheed and Ward, 1948),

p. 289.

[89]*Adulterous Marriages,* i. 9ff.

[90]A. Lehmkuhl, "Divorce," *The Catholic Encyclopedia* (New York: Universal Knowledge Foundation, 1937), Vol. V, p. 56.

[91]Matt. 12:4.

[92]F. E. Gigot, *op. cit.,* pp. 171, 178ff., 221; T. Zahn, *Das Evangelium des Mattheas* (Leipzig: A Deichertsche Verlagsbuchhandlung, 1922), p. 241; Patrick O'Mahony; *Catholics and Divorce* (New York: Thomas Nelson and Sons, 1958), p. 13.

[93]Bruce Vawter, *op. cit.,* p. 164.

[94]*Adulterous Marriages,* i. 9 f.

[95]M. J. Lagrange, *op. cit.,* p. 105 f.

[96]G. H. Box and Charles Gore, *Divorce in the New Testament* (London: S.P.C.K., 1921), p. 32; I. Abrahams, *op. cit.,* p. 71; U. Holsmeister, "Die Streitfrage über die Ehescheidungstext bei Matthäus 5.32, 19.9," *Biblica,* XXVI (1945), p. 135.

[97]John Murray, *Divorce* (Philadelphia: Orthodox Presbyterian Church, 1953), p. 40.

[98]Bruce Vawter, *op. cit.,* p. 162.

[99]Francis Gigot, *op. cit.,* p. 179.

[100]*Ibid.,* p. 221. Cf. David Daube, "Concessions to Sinfulness in Jewish Law," *Journal of Jewish Studies,* X (London, 1959), pp. 1-13.

[101]Deut. 24:4.

[102]Bruce Vawter, *op. cit.,* p. 162.

[103]Joseph Bonsirven, *Le Divorce, op. cit.,* p. 46.

[104]Fernand Prat, *Life of Jesus Christ, op. cit.,* p. 81; U. Holzmeister, *op. cit.,* p. 40; Anton Ott, *Die Ehescheidung in Matthäus-Evangelium* (Würzburg: Ritz-Verlag und Druckerei, 1939), p. 35.

[105]II Cor. 2:13.

[106]Lk. 3:20; Eph. 3:20, 6:16; Col. 3:14.

[107]Bruce Vawter, *op. cit.,* p. 160.

[108]*Ibid.,* p. 161.

[109]Acts. 26:29.

[110]II Cor. 11:28.

[111]II Cor. 11:25-27.

[112]U. Holzmeister, *op. cit.,* p. 138.

[113]Joseph Bonsirven, *Le Divorce, op. cit.,* p. 59; Fernand Prat,

Life of Jesus Christ, op. cit., p. 81; Bruce Vawter, *op. cit.*, p. 162.

[114]Kirsopp Lake, *op. cit.*, p. 140; Oral Colling, "Divorce in the New Testament," *The Gordon Review,* VII (1964), pp. 158-169.

[115]Joseph Bonsirven, *Le Divorce, op. cit.*, p. 50.

[116]Maimonides, *Tractate Issoure bi'a,* xviii. 1-5; cf. M. Yeb. 6.5 and Yeb. 61.

[117]Acts 15:28-29.

[118]I Cor. 5:1-2.

[119]Heb. 12:16.

[120]Gen. 26:34, 35; 27:4.

[121]Bruce Vawter, *op. cit.*, p. 163.

[122]Matt. 9:3-9.

[123]Matt. 5:31-32.

[124]Matt. 5:34.

[125]Matt. 26:63.

[126]H. A. W. Meyer, *Critical and Exegetical Handbook of the Gospel of Matthew,* trans. Peter Christe (New York: Funk and Wagnall, 1884), p. 132.

[127]M. Keth. 3.4-5; Sanh. 52b; J. Sotah 1.1.16b.

[128]R. H. Charles, *op. cit.*, pp. 27-31; R. H. Charles, *Divorce and the Roman Dogma of Nullity* (Edinburgh: T. and T. Clark, 1927), pp. 36-41.

[129]Gen. 38:24.

[130]Hos. 1:2; 3:1.

[131]Acts 15:20, 29, 25; I Cor. 6:13; 6:18; 7:2; Gal. 5:19; Eph. 5:3.

[132]I Cor. 5:1.

[133]*Commentary on Matthew,* xiv.

[134]F. H. Chase, *op. cit.*, p. 42.

[135]*Adulterous Marriages,* xxv.

[136]I Cor. 7:12-16.

[137]Jer. 3:8; 5:7; Ezek. 23:37; 23:43.

[138]Matt. 12:39; 16:4; Mk. 8:38; James 4:4.

[139]I Cor. 7:1-2.

[140]I Cor. 7:8-10.

[141]I Cor. 7:10-11.

[142]I Cor. 7:12-16.

[143]A. Robertson and A. Plummer, *op. cit.*, p. 140.

[144]Fernand Prat, *Theology of St. Paul, op. cit.*, p. 112.
[145]I Cor. 7:14.
[146]Ezek. 10:10.
[147]M. Gitt. 9.8.
[148]R. H. Charles, *Teaching, op. cit.*, p. 60.
[149]David Daube, *op cit.*, p. 362.
[150]I Cor. 7:11.
[151]A. Robertson and A. Plummer, *op. cit.*, p. 143; Augustine, *Adulterous Marriages* i. 13; S. L. Tyson, *The Teaching of our Lord as to the Indissolubility of Marriage* (Sewanee: The University Press, 1909), p. 83; T. P. Considine, "The Pauline Privilege," *Australasian Catholic Record,* XL (*Sydney,* 1963), pp. 107-119.
[152]C. T. Craig, *op. cit.*, p. 80.
[153]O. D. Wakins, *Holy Matrimony, op. cit.*, p. 439 f; R. H. Charles, Teaching, *op. cit.*, p. 60; John Murray, *op. cit.*, p. 76, n. 12; J. J. O'Rourke, "A Note on an Exception: Mt. 5:32 (19:9) and I Cor. 7:12 Compared," *Heythrop Journal,* V (Oxford, 1964), pp. 299-302; Robert Campbell, "Teaching of Paul Concerning Divorce," *Foundations* VI (1963), pp. 363-366.
[154]M. Gitt. 9.3.
[155]A. Robertson and A. Plummer, *op. cit.*, p. 143; F. W. Groselde, *op. cit.*, p. 166.
[156]John Murray, *op. cit.*, p. 76; G. H. Joyce, *op. cit.*, p. 471.
[157]John 4:1-42.
[158]I Tim. 5:9.
[159]I Tim. 3:2.
[160]Morton Scott Enslin, *The Ethics of Paul* (New York: Harper and Brothers, 1930), p. 172.
[161]I Cor. 5:12.
[162]I Cor. 7:15-24.
[163]Gen. 9:1-7.
[164]George F. Moore, *op. cit.*, Vol. I, p. 274 f.
[165]Isa. 24:5.
[166]I Cor. 11:25; Mk. 14:24.
[167]Heb. 8:13; 9:15; II Cor. 3:6.
[168]Gal. 3:27-29.
[169]Eph. 2:12.
[170]Acts 15:20.

[171]Rom. 1:18-32.
[172]Rom. 2:12-16.
[173]Acts 17:24-27.
[174]I Cor. 11:1-16.
[175]Rom. 2:22.
[176]Mk. 7:21-22.
[177]Matt. 5:27-30.
[178]*Ibid.*
[179]Matt. 21:31.
[180]I Cor. 5:11; 6:9; Gal. 5:19-20; Eph. 5:3; Col. 3:5-8.
[181]I Tim. 1:9.
[182]Heb. 13:4.
[183]Rev. 21:8; 22:15.
[184]I Pet. 4:3; Tit. 3:3.
[185]I Cor. 6:15.
[186]A. Robertson and A. Plummer, *op. cit.*, p. 122.
[187]William Graham Cole, *Sex and Love in the Bible* (New York: Association Press, 1959), p. 315 f.
[188]Rev. 17.
[189]Rev. 21:8.
[190]I Cor. 5:1-5.
[191]Rom. 1:26-27.
[192]I Cor. 6:9.
[193]I Tim. 1:9.
[194]Jude 7; Pet. 2:14.
[195]Mk. 10:12.
[196]Matt. 5:27; 5:32; 19:9; Mk. 10:9; Lk. 16:8; 18:20.
[197]I Cor. 6:9.
[198]I. Abrahams, *op. cit.*, p. 73; R. H. Charles, *Teaching, op. cit.*, p. 99.
[199]Rom. 7:1-3.
[200]Rom. 2:22; 13:9.
[201]I Cor. 6:9.
[202]Eph. 5:7-14; II Cor. 6:17.
[203]I Cor. 7:2.
[204]I Cor. 5:9-11.
[205]I Cor. 6:11.
[206]Morton Scott Enslin, *op. cit.*, p. 155.

CHAPTER V

MARRIAGE AND DIVORCE IN THE ANTE-NICENE CHURCH

In this chapter we are concerned with the attitude of the Ante-Nicene Church toward the matter of marriage and divorce. Special attention will be given to the early church's understanding of the New Testament passages and to any new factors, such as the growth of asceticism, which through the spirit of abstinence would modify and shape the church's position. The procedure will be to survey the literature relevant to the various facets of the problem. This will include material from the time of the Apostolic Fathers to the synods and councils held near the beginning of the fourth century.

MARRIAGE

As the New Testament doctrine was influenced by Jewish thought, so the attitude of the Ante-Nicene Church was related to the position of the New Testament. There appears to be no concrete definition of what constitutes marriage. The earliest writers seem to find its essence in the marital union. Thus Tertullian speaks of copulation as the act which makes one woman a wife, makes another woman an adulteress.[1] Clement of Alexandria also sees the sexual consummation as the essential factor in defining marriage.[2] Tertullian, however, in another work refers to contracting marriage "by consenting to its terms."[3] In later writers this idea of consent is made the primary part of matrimony. This development was perhaps theological in nature so as to protect both the marriage and perpetual virginity of Mary.[4] It appears that the Ante-Nicene Church accepted without reflection the current concepts of marriage which existed in the Roman world.

Object of Praise

The passages pertaining to marriage in the Apostolic Fathers have a continuity with the New Testament. Marriage is viewed as honorable and in keeping with the plan of God. Hermas employs more than once the idea that Christ is the bridegroom and the church is the bride.[5] Such a figure of speech could only have been employed if marriage were esteemed. Clement of Rome suggests that Christians marry because God commands man to increase and multiply.[6] The same idea is expressed by the anonymous author of the *Epistle of Diognetus*, where in contrasting Christian conduct with pagan, he says, "They marry as all men, they bear children, but do not expose their offspring."[7] Justin Martyr also affirms that the followers of Jesus may marry and that their purpose in so doing is to bring up children.[8] Elsewhere he stresses that every Christian has his own wife, which indicates the acceptability of matrimony.[9] The very same argument is made by Athenagoras, although he does admit that some forego the right of marriage.[10] Tertullian, in his *Treatise on the Soul,* goes further in an excursus in which he defends his frankness in writing, insisting that it is "lust, not natural usage, which brought shame on the intercourse of the sexes."[11] He continues by saying that the normal marital sexual relation was blessed by God.[12] Marriage as a divinely ordained institution was often defended. Methodius viewed it as a cooperating with God in forming the image of the creator.[13] Theophilus makes the same point.[14] Tertullian saw all hostile attacks against marriage as a disparagement of the Creator.[15] This is a frequent charge that Tertullian makes in his writings against the gnostic view. Clement of Alexandria makes sport of the prohibition made against marriage by Marcion, who was opposed to peopling the world of the God-Creator, although he did not prohibit food and air which were also provided by the same deity.[16] Clement quotes the words of Paul who warned that some would prohibit marriage. In his most direct statements, Clement claims that, "if the law is holy, marriage is holy."[17] The honor in which marriage was held was not easily set aside in later times even by the growing ideal of asceticism. This is indicated at the very close of the period covered by this investigation. When the Council of Nicea heard aspersions cast upon the institution of matrimony by the advocates of celibacy for the priesthood, they supported the aged Paphnutius who reminded the assembly that marriage was an honorable estate.[18]

Religious nature of marriage.—Perhaps the high regard in which marriage was held is no better seen than in the religious aura which surrounds such unions in some of the Fathers. Not that at this early period it was viewed as a sacrament,[19] but the germinal idea for the later doctrine was already planted. The earliest reference which reflects this tendency comes from Ignatius, who urged that marriage should only be contracted with the approval of the bishop.[20] Something of the same spirit is reflected by Tertullian. While contemplating the bliss of marriage, Tertullian, perhaps for the first time, is at a loss for words.

> How shall we ever be able adequately to describe the happiness of that marriage which the Church arranges, the Sacrifice strengthens, upon which the blessing sets a seal, at which angels are present as witness, and to which the Father gives his consent.[21]

The background for the remarks of Ignatius and Tertullian is to be found in the ceremony and custom of marriage existing in their larger environment. In the Roman marriage custom there was a person, called a conciliator,[22] who arranged the union. Apparently in the eyes of both writers the corresponding role was played by the church. In the course of a Roman marriage there was both a sacrifice and a sealing placed on the written certificate. In the African's view both of these were done by God for the Christian. Just how this was performed by God or by the church is not clear in the literature. But this appears to be more than a convenient parallel for Tertullian. He writes, "For not even on earth do children marry properly and legally without their Father's permission."[23] Thus he implies that Christians must have their heavenly Father's consent. Elsewhere he speaks of a wife who is converted to the faith as having the obligation to persevere in her marriage to her pagan husband, for it has a "partial sanction of divine grace."[24] Origen considers both marriage and celibacy as graces.

> And it is God who has joined together the two in one so that they are no more twain, from the time that the woman is married to the man. And, since God has joined them together, on this account in the care of those who are joined together by God, there is a "gift"; and Paul knowing this, that marriage according to the word of God was a "gift" like as holy celibacy was a gift, says, "But I would that all men were like myself; howbeit, each man hath his own gift from God, one after this manner, and another after that."[25]

Clement of Alexandria also believed that there was the added gift of sanctification if the union was in subjection to God.[26]

It appears that during this period of the church's history the Roman law and custom of marriage was accepted without change. The only possible innovation would be the prayer or benediction at the ceremony. Clement, in speaking of women wearing wigs, asks: "In such a case, on whom does the priest lay his hands? Whom does he bless?"[27] Specific references to this practice do not appear until the Post-Nicene period. Certainly the church did not exercise jurisdiction over Christian marriages. It is significant that Joyce begins his discussion of "The Church's Jurisdiction Over Matrimony Causes"[28] with the collapse of the Western Empire and the influence of the German tribes. This is not to say that the church was unconcerned.

> Marriage is, in the first place, an affair of the family. In the earliest period the Christian congregation regarded itself as a spiritual family, and the life and concerns of every member of the congregation were of intimate interest to the whole body.[29]

It would seem that marriage, like other established institutions, was dealt with by the church laying down broad principles.[30] An analogy to the church's indifference to the wedding ceremony can be found in the church's attitude toward the institution of slavery.[31] Neither case called for revolution. The only hint as to why the church was unconcerned with the marriage ceremony comes from Tertullian. For him the institution of marriage was governed by eschatology.[32]

Form of Marriage

Concerning the form of Christian marriage, there has never been any doubt. Marriage was for the followers of

Jesus a monogamous relationship. Practically every writer in the early church who had an occasion on which to mention morals, discusses the matter of monogamy. Justin speaks of Christians having their own wives,[33] and chides the Jews for allowing each man to have four or five wives.[34] Theophilus sees some correlation between monogamy and monotheism.[35] Origen[36] and Athenagoras[37] both assume a single union. Clement of Alexandria, when contrasting the old and new covenants, assigns single marriages to the present age.[38] Tertullian devotes one of his tracts to the subject of *Monogamy* in which he advocates the monogamous relationship against both polygamy and consecutive polygamy, or digamy. In making his case he points out that the animals went into the ark two by two,[39] a Jewish argument which has already been noticed.[40] Tertullian reflects here a common approach of the Fathers in appealing to nature to support their position. He, for example, is careful to appeal to the habits of birds in support of monogamy. He employs another argument in the *Letter to his Wife* by reminding her that monogamy is indicated by the fact that God took only one rib from man to make woman.[41] In his *Apology* the same author, having called attention to pagan vices, stresses that a Christian man has "nothing to do with any but his own wife."[42] It is Methodius who starts with the departure from the first couple and sees the monogamy of the Christian system as an evolution:

. . . that first they should abandon the intermar-

> riage of brothers and sisters, and marry wives from other families; and then they should no longer have many wives, like brute beasts, as though born for the mere propagation of species; and then that they should not be adulterers; and then again that they should go on to continence, and from continence, to virginity, when having trained themselves to despise the flesh, they sail fearlessly into the peaceful haven of immortality.[43]

Interestingly enough, Methodius appeals to the sexual habits of animals as examples of sensuality, while the other Fathers appeal to nature to support monogamy. Lactantius protests, against the view of some, that concubinage was not an indication of polygamy, but only a kind of adjunct to monogamy.[44] In an earlier passage he also condemns Plato for advocating a community of goods, including wives. On the whole, in both ideal and practice, the early Church was strongly opposed to any form of polygamy. It is true that some sects practiced a community of goods, including wives, but those who did so were far removed from the main stream of Christianity.[45]

Depreciation of Marriage

At an early date there arose in the Ante-Nicene Church a tendency to depreciate marriage. Undoubtedly many sources contributed to this spirit. A Platonic synthesis began to filter into the Church,[46] as did the dualism exemplified in the Manichean position.[47] In addition, in the Church's theology the doctrine of redemption was stressed to the slighting of the doctrine of creation.[48] The loss of a theological equilibrium began to point toward asceticism. Also there was on the part of the normative churches a deep moral reaction against the depravity exemplified in the world.[49] Although the impetus for these movements came from different sources, they all sought a biblical basis for the practice of asceticism. The movement found expression in attempts to regulate, restrain, and finally reject certain marriages.

Continence in Marriage.—The first serious step in the revaluation of matrimony was the insistence that sexual relations were only for the purpose of procreation. In the second century Athenagoras assured his readers that marriage among Christians was "only for the purpose of having children."[50] Justin likewise sought to disassociate the Christian from any charge of lust by affirming that the purpose of marriage was the rearing of children.[51] It was, however, Clement of Alexandria who was the most candid writer on the subject. A favorite analogy with him was the figure of a farmer sowing seed. "Sowing seed," he says, "is permissible only for the husband . . . and even for him only when the season is favorable for sowing."[52] Elsewhere he appeals to the idea that a husband is a co-worker with God in creation and should not purposely engage in futile work.[53] In fact, relations without the intention of begetting children are to the Alexandrian an outrage. In addition to the various factors at work which produced the ascetic spirit, this attitude of limiting sexual relations to procreation may have been the most important idea. Bailey[54] suggests that this prejudice was the result of a misunderstanding on the part of the Fathers of the process of procreation. It was a common belief in the ancient world that the semen also had the properties of the fertilized ovum, that is, the semen provided the process while the woman merely provided the place for growth. Thus part of the patristic concern with the procreation of children as the only reason for sexual relations was because they viewed the "wasteful" sowing of the seed as abortion or infanticide—the taking of human life. The Fathers would have been especially sensitive since infanticide was a recurring charge brought against the early Christians by the pagans.

Restraint of Marriage.—The most frequent and best known indication of the depreciation of marriage is that of voluntary celibacy. This esteem for abstinence also appears at a very early date in the patristic writings. Both Clement of Rome[55] and Ignatius[56] deemed it necessary to warn that celibacy should be practiced without boasting. Athenagoras[57] and Tertullian,[58] however, take a good deal of pride in the fact that some Christians remained virgins throughout life. Nearly all the Fathers extol virginity as a special gift from God. All the apostles, with the exception of Peter, were virgins, Tertullian believed.[59] In the view of Origen, virgins were the flowers which adorned the Church,[60] and the celibate state was superior to marriage.[61] Tertullian went to great lengths to show that marriage is a relative good and that abstinence is better.[62] In his montanistic days he referred, in his acid style, to the desire for progeny that prompts people to marry as the "bitter pleasure of children."[63] As might be guessed, this great enemy of marriage was himself married. To advocate the celibate life placed the advocates in the uncomfortable position of having also to depreciate God's command to "multiply and replenish the earth." Flagley[64] finds the patristic attitude toward parenthood was shaped in part by the feeling that the end was near. Tertullian[65] and his successor, Cyprian,[66] set aside the command on the grounds that the earth is filled with people and that the end, therefore, is at hand. Virginity finds its greatest champion, however, in Methodius. There is a poetic exaltation of abstinence in his *Banquet of the Ten Virgins*. There he sees virginity as the apex of an evolution of sexual morality which has developed through polygamy and monogamy to continence and chastity.[67] Virginity is the crown and summation of all virtues.[68] Even in etymology Methodius finds an argument to bolster his position. By the changing of one letter, he indicates, "virgin" becomes "divine" (παρθενία becomes παρθεία).[69]

The Fathers said clearly that such continence was impossible for all Christians; in this they followed Paul's position in I Corinthians 7. Clement of Rome reminds the Corinthians "that it is another who bestows . . . continence."[70] Clement of Alexandria agrees with his predecessor that it is God's gift.[71] Some who had not received the gift apparently tried to secure the same end through emasculation. Justin Martyr speaks with seeming approval of a Christian who sought, although unsuccessfully, to acquire governmental permission to have himself castrated.[72] Also there comes to mind the well known case of Origen who availed himself of this means of escape. In addition, there is a statement that Melito, one of the illustrious leaders of the church in Asia, was a eunuch, although it is not clear whether he became such after he accepted Christianity; nor are other details available.[73] The practice of emasculation apparently grew to such proportions that Clement of Alexandria felt it necessary to remind his readers that the true eunuchs for the Kingdom of heaven's sake were not those who were unable to lust, but those who would not lust.[74] Originally abstinence was associated with the laity and not with the clergy, as is often assumed by laymen. When marriage came to be viewed as religiously the second best situation, it was natural that abstinence came to be identified also with the clergy. An aspect of this was the similarity of the various grades of the Christian ministry to Jewish and heathen priesthoods and a desire for holiness which found expression in the demand placed upon the Christian ministers for a higher degree of sanctity than was to be found among others.[75] In general, however, the process of the development of clerical celibacy was gradual.[76] Tertullian was concerned that a priest who is a digamist should be permitted to fulfill his religious duties.[77] The matter was openly discussed in the Council of Nicea where an effort was made to prohibit the married clergy from cohabitating with their wives. This motion was defeated, according to Socrates, largely through the influence of Paphnutius. This respected older churchman made his case by insisting that marriage was honorable, that all men could not abstain, and that the enforced abstinence of the priests might expose their wives to unchastity.[78] The prohibition of marriage to the clergy in the West, and its restriction in the East, transpired at a period beyond the scope of this investigation, but it had advanced considerably toward these later positions by the end of the fourth century.

Spiritual Marriages.—Spiritual marriages, or sexless unions, were also the result of the tendency to depreciate normal marriages. Such an ascetic union is alluded to by Hermas who advocates treating a wife as a sister.[79] In another place the Shepherd, who is a patrician of the celibate state, refers to spending the night with a group of maidens "as a brother and not as a husband."[80] Tertullian, in speaking of the lusts of the flesh and in referring to the matter of digamy, condemns a man using as a pretext for a second marriage the need for domestic help by suggesting that the man should take a widow as his spiritual wife. As an added inducement, Tertullian reminds a spiritual husband that by this arrangement it is possible to have several wives.[81] The same author is equally frank when he advises a widower who is lonely and therefore contemplating a second marriage, to avail himself of a widow as a spiritual wife.[82] This practice apparently had some acceptability in the Church for it is mentioned also by Irenaeus,[83] and by Cyprian.[84] According to Eusebius,[85] Paul of Samosata practiced spiritual marriage and it was the abuse of such unions that provided the grounds, in part, for criticism of the Antiochian leader. Heretical groups, according to hostile writers, practiced similar unions. Such was the case with the Valentians,[86] Montanists,[87] and Marcionites.[88] Among such unions with virgins or widows, scandals, either real or imagined, were bound to arise. Cyprian laments the news that some virgins not only lived, but also slept with Christian men. He further cries against the "multitude of virgins we behold corrupted by unlawful and dangerous conjunctions of this kind."[89] Cyprian also provides detailed instructions as to what should be done with the offending individuals. The practice of spiritual marriage was so open to abuse and placed such a strain of temptation on the participants that it eventually fell into general disrepute. The Synods of Elvira,[90] Ancyra,[91] and Nicea[92] all concurred in condemnation of the practice.

Condemned Marriages.—The disparagement of marriage found its ultimate expression in the condemnation of marriage. In some circumstances the church, during the Ante-Nicene period, not only discouraged certain unions, but actually condemned others.

A second marriage after the death of the original mate was condemned. It has already been indicated that such was the popular attitude in Roman society.[93] Digamy is condemned in Hermas,[94] and is a sin in the eyes of Justin

Martyr.[95] Athenagoras termed it "specious adultery."[96] The matter of digamy receives its fullest treatment by Tertullian. In his montanist stage, he equates it with bigamy.[97] With characteristic sarcasm, he pictures the plight of a man who had two wives—one living, the other dead. Which one, he desires to know, will the husband pray for?[98] The objection to remarriage was that it was a concession to man's carnal nature and ignoble motives, such as concupiscence or ambition.[99] In part, the objection was also rooted in the idea that marriage transcended death.[100] Tertullian recognized that the continence required of widows was far greater than that required of virgins, and it is the former that receive the greater honor.[101] The only concession that Tertullian makes, although it is a highly significant one, is that if they were widowed before they became Christians, then it was permissible to remarry. The approach of Clement of Alexandria to the problem is a more moderate one. Although he frowns on second marriages, he recognizes that they are inevitable.[102] Origen also presents a temperate position. While he suggests that couples take vows that they will not remarry, he believes a digamist will still be saved, although he held that a digamist would not be crowned.[103] This obviously creates a group of second-rate Christians. Callistus, Bishop of Rome, permitted second marriages, but his attitude on matrimonial matters was often out of harmony with the normative position.[104] The Council of Nicea also affirmed the lawfulness of digamy, but this was formulated in the face of the

Novatians who categorically denied the validity of digamist unions.

Mixed marriages, that is between a Christian and a non-Christian, were condemned. If the teaching concerning second marriages was ignored, the only possibility for marriage was with a fellow Christian. None of the Fathers mentions mixed marriages between Christians and heretics; it is always between Christians and pagans.[105] Marriage between an individual who was already a Christian and a non-Christian was condemned,[106] although such unions are reflected in both Tertullian[107] and Cyprian.[108] If one were married before conversion, the marriage was valid and was to be continued.[109] The requirements placed by the Fathers on second marriages resulted in placing some Christians at a distinct disadvantage. This was especially true of Christians of rank. Women of high rank were not allowed by Roman law to contract marriages with men of lower birth—either freedmen or slaves, although Roman law did accept a concubinage arrangement in such cases. Callistus, Bishop of Rome, was willing in his church to accept such morganatic unions as the equivalent of marriage, thereby making it possible to keep the ideal that second marriages be only with fellow Christians.[110]

DIVORCE

Christians, like other individuals in the Empire, had the legal right of divorce. Under Roman law, as has been previously indicated, marriage was viewed as a private contract, and like other contracts, could be dissolved. The dissolution could be either at the instigation of one party or by mutual consent, the only crucial requirement being that it be made in the presence of seven adult witnesses. In most cases it was not necessary to go to law, the exceptions being in grave matters, such as adultery, where there was a civil penalty attached and the courts were involved.[111] Even when Roman law came under the control of Christian influence, as in the time of Constantine, no sweeping revisions were made in the matter of divorce.[112] Consequently, divorce was not difficult to obtain. The same laws which provided for easy divorce also encouraged remarriage since heavy fines were imposed on single individuals by the state.

The frequency with which Christians availed themselves of this right of divorce provided by the state is not indicated by the material available. The discussion of divorce among patristic writers would seem to indicate that the matter of divorce was no theoretical question. Lactantius, in describing the Diocletian persecutions, speaks of an edict which debarred Christians from being plaintiffs "in questions of wrong, adultery, or theft."[113] Adultery was one of the grave wrongs which involved a penalty on the guilty person and it was necessary to establish the adultery in court if it were the grounds for the divorce. This reference would suggest that adultery, at least, was the basis upon which some Christians were obtaining divorces. Especially suggestive in ascertaining the reality of Christians divorcing their mates is the period immediately following the Ante-Nicene Church. Chrysostom remarked that there were some in his congregation who hung their heads in shame whenever he preached on divorce.[114] Ambrose warned his readers against availing themselves of the civil laws.[115] It was Augustine who devoted most space to the subject, making it the theme of *On Adulterous Marriages.* While these examples fall outside the area of investigation of this book, there is no reason to suppose that divorce suddenly appeared as a unique problem after the time of Constantine. In all probability divorce remained a common solution to marital problems, and divorce in the Roman world grew gradually into a problem within the church as the church grew and received the political blessings of the Emperor.

Grounds for Divorce

The references in patristic writings to divorce can be classified according to the attitude presented in them toward the doctrine of divorce and remarriage as reflected in the New Testament. Some passages would seem to indicate that divorce is impossible; others mention the exception clause found in Matthew's Gospel; other statements make no mention of the exception clause and are not clear about the possibility of divorce and remarriage; and finally one category seems to indicate that divorce and remarriage are possible on grounds other than the "adultery" of the exception clause.

Divorce Unacceptable.— There is considerable evidence that many in the Ante-Nicene Church considered divorce, regardless of grounds, as unacceptable for a Christian.

Authors.—The first literary reference that would indicate that divorce was unacceptable, even in the case of adultery, comes from the Shepherd of Hermas. Hermas had the Shepherd inquire of the angel about what the course of conduct which a husband, who divorces his wife because of her adultery, should be. The angel replied:

> Let him put her away and let the husband remain by himself. But if he puts his wife away and marries another he also commits adultery himself.[116]

The Shepherd then asked if the husband had the responsibility to receive the wife back in case she repented. To this the angel replied:

> Yes, if the husband does not receive her he sins and covers himself with a great sin; but it is necessary to receive the sinner who repents, but not often, for the servant of God has but one repentance. Therefore, for the sake of repentance the husband ought not to remarry.[117]

A second passage which is similar in tone to Hermas is from the montanistic writings of Tertullian. In his treatise on *Monogamy* he wrote:

> A divorced woman is not able even to marry legitimately, and if she attempts some sort of union which is not marriage, will she not be guilty of the charge of adultery, seeing that adultery is an offense

> against marriage? . . .
>
> It is unreasonable, therefore, to argue that whereas God does not wish a divorced woman to marry a second time if her husband is living, He consents to it if her husband is dead, since if she is not bound to a husband who is dead, no more is she bound to one who is living . . . They [Romans] committed adultery, however, although they did not divorce; we, on the contrary, do not even permit remarriage, though we do allow divorce.[118]

The argument of Tertullian is that if divorce does not free a Christian for another marriage, it should not be considered that death frees a Christian for a digamist union. The remark, "We, on the contrary, do not even permit remarriage, though we do allow divorce," is modified by some other factors. He introduces this discussion by quoting from Matthew 5:32 and mentioning the exception clause. It is possible, therefore, in speaking of the impossibility of remarriage, that he is referring to those circumstances which fall outside the exception of "adultery." Another ambiguous passage is found in another of Tertullian's works where he personifies Patience.

> . . . when, on a disjunction of wedlock (for that cause, I mean, which makes it lawful, whether for the husband or wife, to persist in the perpetual observance of widowhood), she waits for, she yearns for, she persuades by her entreaties, repentance in all who are one day to enter salvation? How great a blessing she confers on each. The one she prevents

from becoming an adulterer; the other she amends.[119] The interpretation hinges on the meaning of what it is that permits an accepted separation. Is it the adultery of the exception clause? Perhaps it is a mixed marriage with a pagan which in another place the North African calls "adultery."[120]

The third author to write similarly to Hermas and Tertullian was Clement of Alexandria. In the closing of the second book of the *Stromata*, he states:

> Now that the scriptures counsel marriage, and allow no release from the union, is expressly contained in the law, "Thou shalt not put away thy wife, except for the cause of fornication"; and it regards as fornication, the marriage of those separated while the other is alive.[121]

This can be taken as prohibiting the remarriage of the innocent party even in the circumstance of adultery. Thus he would interpret Jesus' words as permitting separation from bed and board, but not as also extending the right to remarry. On the other hand, it is possible to limit the prohibition of remarriage only to those who have divorced for some other reason than the "adultery" of the exception clause. The probability of this is increased by Clement's further remarks in the same context.

> And not only is he who puts her away guilty of this, but he who takes her, by giving to the woman the opportunity of sinning; for if he did not take her, she would return to her husband.[122]

As has already been indicated, both the remarks of

Tertullian and Clement are amenable to interpretations which would limit them to prohibiting remarriage only to those who have divorced illegally. In addition, it is striking that both of these writers and Hermas included in the context prohibiting remarriage statements pertaining to a possible reconciliation of the estranged couple. The angel tells the Shepherd, "For the sake of repentance the husband ought not to remarry."[123] Tertullian, in extolling Patience, says that when a person enters the observance of perpetual widowhood, he is brought by Patience to repentance and the innocent party is thereby saved from adulterous remarriage and the guilty is brought to make amends.[124] Clement, in discussing the remarriage of a divorced person, says, "For if he did not take her, she would return to her husband."[125] It is perhaps too strong to suggest that this hope of reconciliation and the church's doctrine of limited repentance were responsible for the spirit which prohibited divorce and the right to remarry even in cases of adultery, but it is a possibility about which more will be said later. The situation is also modified by the fact that in both Tertullian and Clement remarks occur which would seem to indicate that they deemed it possible to remarry after a divorce on the grounds of adultery. In Tertullian's earlier writings against Marcion he counters the argument of Marcion that the God of the Christians is different from the God of the Old Testament by a specific reference to divorce. Marcion believed that in the matter of divorce it could be seen that they were not the same divine being because in the Old Testament divorce was possible while in the New Testament it was prohibited. Tertullian replied:

> I maintain, then, that there was a condition in the prohibition which He now made of divorce; the case supposed being, that a man put away his wife for the express purpose of marrying another. His words are: "Whosoever putteth away his wife, and marrieth another, committeth adultery; and whosoever marrieth her that is put away from her husband, also committeth adultery,"—"put away," that is, dismissed, that another wife may be obtained. For he that marries a woman who is unlawfully put away is as much of an adulterer as the man who marries one who is undivorced. Permanent is the marriage which is not rightly dissolved; to marry, therefore, whilst matrimony is undissolved, is to commit adultery.[126]

The entire tenor of this passage is to suggest that divorce and remarriage are possible under proper conditions. These words of Tertullian provide an extreme difficulty for those who are committed to maintaining the impossibility of divorce with the correlative right to remarry. Joyce suggests that Tertullian in his answer "overshoots the mark."[127] Luckock sees no explanation other than to say that Tertullian is inconsistent."[128] Even if it is granted that while Tertullian was a Montanist he denied the possibility of divorce and remarriage, Tertullian only means that he had become more of a rigorist since his earlier days. A similar hardening of the doctrines can be discerned in his position toward digamy.

In the third book of the *Stromata*, Clement makes a statement which also suggests that he accepted the possibility of divorce and remarriage. In commenting on the words of Jesus, he says:

> After his words about divorce some asked him whether, if that is the position in relation to women, it is better not to marry; and it was then that the Lord said; "Not all can receive this saying, but those to whom it is granted." What the questioners wanted to know was whether, when a man's wife has been condemned for fornication, it is allowable for him to marry another.[129]

In relating the remarks about adultery and divorce directly with the matter of being eunuchs, Clement implies that for those who do not have the gift of being a eunuch it is permissible to remarry.

Synods.—In addition to the testimony of the individual Fathers, there is the witness of two synods on the problem of divorce.

The Synod of Elvira was conducted in that Spanish town probably in the beginning of the fourth century. The Spanish Church was, of course, well represented and among the signers was Hosius of Cordova, who was later to become famous in the Arian controversy. The primary concern of the Synod was the state of the lapsed, and also to seek for means to prevent moral corruption.[130] The eighth and ninth canons of that Synod are especially pertinent. They are respectively as follows:

> Women who without any precedent cause have left their husbands and joined themselves to others, may not have communion even at the last.[131]

> A Christian woman who has left an adulterous Christian husband and married another, must be forbidden to do so; but if she has married, she may not receive communion till he whom she has left be dead; unless some mortal sickness compel one to give it to her.[132]

The ninth canon taken by itself would imply that divorce was not possible for Christians even for adultery. But the ninth canon must be interpreted in the light of the eighth. It is seen when they are compared that the Synod made a distinction between those who divorced and remarried "without any precedent cause" and those who divorced and remarried because of an "adulterous husband." The former is not permitted communion even at death; the latter is forbidden communion unless death is near. If the church prohibited divorce and subsequent remarriage, regardless of circumstances, it is difficult to see why it was sympathetic, to however minor a degree, to a situation involving adultery. It is easier to imagine that the excommunication of the innocent party was merely an expression of rigorism growing within the church, but not yet strong enough to disregard the exception clause of Matthew and the permission to remarry as expressed in some patristic writings.

Another relevant Synod was the one held in Gaul in the town of Arles in the year 314. The representatives of most of Western Christendom, including the Donatist party, were present.[133] The primary concern of the Synod was with the Donatist situation, but the tenth canon pertains to the matter of divorce.

> Concerning those baptized Christians who detect their wives in adultery, who are also young men, and are forbidden to remarry, it is resolved, that counsel as strong as possible be given them, that so long as their wives are alive, although in adultery, they should not marry others.[134]

The phrase "and are forbidden to remarry" would seem to indicate that remarriage was not possible even on the grounds of adultery, which would reduce divorce technically to separation. It is interesting to compare this canon with the two from the Synod of Elvira. In the latter it is a Christian woman who divorces her husband for adultery and remarries. She is denied communion unless gravely ill. In the Synod of Arles it is the Christian man who divorces his adulterous wife. While he is "forbidden" to remarry, it is envisioned that the young man might well remarry and in such circumstances "strong" counsel is to be given in an attempt to dissuade him. It seems strange that the only corrective approach sanctioned by the Synod is the matter of strong counsel, and there is no mention, as in the Synod of Elvira, of excommunication. This does not render impossible the view that, while the church in its rigorism forbade second marriages, such unions were still formed without excommunication of the participants.

Second Repentance.—It is now appropriate to discuss more fully the factor which undoubtedly affected the Ante-Nicene Church's rigorism and prejudice against re-marriage after divorce for the innocent party, that is, the doctrine of repentance. It was generally held that the church of this period recognized only one opportunity to repent of sins after baptism and that some sins, notably murder, idolatry and adultery, while they were removable through repentance, were of such a nature that those guilty of them could not be received back into active relationship with the church.[135] These would only be forgiven the sinners in the day of judgment by God.[136] The doctrine of second repentance is summarized by Tertullian.

> Accordingly, since God foresees this virulence of his (Devil), He has permitted the door of forgiveness, although it is closed and locked by the bar of Baptism, still to stand somewhat open. He has placed in the vestibule a second penitence so that it may open the door to those who knock; only once, however, because it is already a second time; never again, however, because the last time was in vain. For is not even this "once" enough?[137]

This rigorist position regarding the crimes of murder,

adultery, and idolatry had largely won in the church by the second and third centuries.[138] Ireneaus, in discussing the gnostic Marcus, speaks of receiving into the church women who were guilty of illegal sexual relations. He mentions specifically a deacon's wife who had been seduced by Marcus as being received.[139] A contemporary of Ireneaus in the East was Dionysius of Corinth. Eusebius quotes Dionysius' appeal to the Bishop of Crete to maintain a more lenient attitude toward breaches of purity and to receive the offenders into the church.[140] The Bishop of Crete, Pinytus, requested stronger food from Dionysius the next time he wrote. Another example of the growing acceptance of rigorism is seen in the circumstances relating to Marcion. According to Epiphanius, Marcion as a young man had violated a virgin of the Church and was expelled from the church at Sinope, where Marcion's father was a bishop. Although Marcion repented and asked readmission to the church, it was denied him by his father. Hermas of Rome bears witness to the same unbending policy; he did not teach that adultery was irremissible, but he maintained that the church could forgive it. Hardly had he adopted the above position, than he found it necessary to defend himself against the charge that he was lax. That he deemed it necessary to defend himself must be some indication of the growing concern with a rigorous attitude. Clement of Alexandria occupies a position similar to Hermas'. He believed that there was one repentance for unwillful sins after baptism, but that included in this single remission was the sin of adultery. He believed the church could deal with adultery. Thus he wrote in the *Stromata*:

> . . . but she who has repented, being as it were born again by the change in her life, has a regeneration of life; the old harlot being dead, and she who has been regenerated by repentance having come back again to life.[141]

A position of some laxity was apparently held by Callistus, the Bishop of Rome. Thus the position of Callistus is presented by his bitterest foe, Hippolytus:

> And he first invented the device of conniving with men in regard to their indulgences in sensual pleasures, saying that all had their sins forgiven by himself . . . This one propounded the opinion, that if a bishop was guilty of any sin, if even a sin unto death, he ought not to be deposed. About the time of this man, bishops, priests, and deacons, who had been twice married, and thrice married, began to be allowed to retain their place among the clergy. If also, however, anyone who is in holy orders should become married, Callistus permitted such a one to continue in holy orders as if he had not sinned.[142]

The action of Callistus also provoked the wrath of Tertullian. In a scathing passage the North African writes:

> I even hear that an Edict has been issued, indeed a peremptory one (nor could I permit it to pass unnoticed), which opposes this rigor. The Pontifex Maximus, forsooth—I mean the "bishop of bishops!"—issues this pronouncement: I forgive sins of adultery and fornication to those who have performed penance.[143]

This pardon of adulterers and fornicators, he continues, is "in opposition to fundamental Christian discipline." Later in the conclusion to the treatise he insists that if adulterers are pardoned, idolaters and murderers should be also.[144] Thus from the middle of the second century rigorism spread in the churches. Tertullian is a witness for Africa, Hippolytus of Rome, Origen of Egypt and Syria, Pinytus of Cnossus of Crete, Irenaeus of Asia Minor and Gaul. But the spirit of rigorism soon began to fade, save possibly in Spain, with the second Carthage Council of 252 and the following synods which were concerned with the lapsed. This change is sharply brought out by Bainton when he says:

> Whereas in A.D. 220 Tertullian could say, "Shall we forgive adulterers when we do not forgive apostates?" In 250 Cyprian could ask, "Shall we refuse to forgive apostates since we do forgive adulterers?[145]

Bainton continues to point out that this relaxation on the part of the church was in marked contrast to the attitude of the state, for this was a period in which adultery received the severest civil punishment. Whereas before this period the forgiveness of adultery was viewed as being beyond the prerogatives of the church and carried therefore the denial of communion, now adultery was deemed reconcilable by the church. This new spirit is exemplified in the work of Gregory the Wonder Worker who devised a graded system of penance. In his epistle he permits, for example, Christian women who have been carried away into captivity and placed in concubinage and about whom there is no doubt as to whether they submitted to this willingly, to be accepted back into the church.[146] This system of gradation of penance found quick acceptance in the East. Thus the Council of Ancyra, meeting in Galatia in A.D. 314, adopted such a system. Its sixteenth canon required that a person guilty of bestiality, if under twenty years of age, was to remain fifteen years among the "Fallers" (one of the grades of the penitents), and five additional years among the "Prayers," before being admitted to communion. If the offense was committed by a young married person, the time among the "Fallers" was raised to twenty-five years. If the person was over fifty, he was only to receive communion again at the approach of death.[147] The Council of Neo-Caesarea held shortly afterward in Cappadocia established the penance for priests guilty of fornication.[148] The third canon sets the duration of penance for individuals who have married several times.

> As for those who have been often married, the duration of their penance is well known; but their good conduct and faith may shorten that period.[149]

This "well known" penance mentioned in the canon is unknown today. It is usually assumed to refer to digamy or trigamy. In later times the penance involved for these might be from one to five years.[150] In the West no system of penance was adopted by the Ante-Nicene Church, but gross laxity toward sexual sins is also indicated. The Synod of Elvira, which has already been discussed, allowed one guilty of adultery to perform the penance and be received back into the Church.[151] Even one who was a frequent adulterer could receive communion at his death bed, if he promised to mend his ways should he recover.[152] If adultery was only committed once the specific penance assigned was five years.[153] If the partner was a Jew or pagan, the penance was still five years, unless it was confessed spontaneously; then the penance period was unspecified, but presumably shorter than the five years.[154] A widow who had relations with a man she later married was required to do five years of penance. If, however, she had relations with one man and married another, she was forbidden to receive communion even on her death bed and the man she married, if he was a Christian, was subject to ten years penance for marrying a woman who was not free.[155] The Synod prohibited a prostitute who sought in some way to destroy any issue of her unions from receiving communion even on her death bed. This relaxing of the attitude toward sexual sins by the Synod of Elvira is probably indicative of a laxer view elsewhere. Elvira, being in Spain, shared the Spanish rigorist reputation. If the Synod of Elvira was this lax, it is safe to assume the rest of the Empire was more lax. The Synod of Ancyra, which met about the same time in the East, also dealt with the matter of prostitutes and subjected them only to ten years of penance.[156]

Exception Not Mentioned.—There are some passages which refer to the matter of divorce but do not mention specifically the exception clause. The first to fall in this category is a passage from Justin Martyr where he gives a summation of Christ's teaching on chastity and quotes from Matthew 5:32.

> "And whosoever shall marry her that is divorced from another husband, committeth adultery." . . . So that all who, by human law are twice married, are in the eye of our Master sinners . . . .[157]

The words 'twice married" (διγαμίας ποιούμενοι) may refer to: (a) bigamy, that is, a man married to a second wife while still married to the first; (b) digamy, that is, a man who marries a second time following the death of his first wife; or (c) a man who marries a second time following the divorce of his first wife. Assuming that Justin refers to the last, this passage cannot be read as a prohibition of remarriage after a divorce. Jesus uses the words, "Whosoever shall marry her that is divorced from another husband, committeth adultery," to refer to someone illegally divorced, that is, for the ground other than "fornication." There is no reason to suppose that Justin is using the words in any different sense than recorded in Matthew. Another relevant passage is from Athenagoras, who merely quotes, "Whosoever shall put away his wife and marry another commits adultery" (Mk. 10:11). Since there is no exception in Mark, there should be no concern that Athenagoras does not employ it here.[158] Cyprian likewise speaks about separation of married couples without mentioning the right of divorce, but his comments are based in I Corinthians 7, which does not mention the exception.[159] These three passages are inadequate as evidence to show conclusively that divorce, with the right of remarriage, was rejected by the category of silent evidence, for their ambiguity can be explained on other terms.

Exception Clause Mentioned.—The exception clause is mentioned by most of the writers who comment upon the subject of divorce, for most take Matthew's Gospel as their main source.[160] The clause is mentioned in Theophilus,[161] Clement of Alexandria,[162] Origen,[163] Tertullian,[164] and Lactantius.[165] In the *Epitome of the Institutes*, a work sometimes ascribed to Lactantius, the author wrote:

> But as a woman is bound by the bonds of chastity not to desire any other man, so let the husband be bound by the same law, since God has joined to-

> gether the husband and wife in the union of one body. On this account He has commanded that the wife shall not be put away unless convicted of adultery, and that the bond of conjugal compact shall never be dissolved, unless unfaithfulness have broken it.[166]

It seems in this passage that the author clearly implies that adultery breaks the bond of matrimony and that therefore the innocent party has the right to remarry. To those who are committed to the position that under no circumstances could the church permit those who had been divorced to remarry, these comments prove to be a difficulty. Luckock handles the problem nicely by challenging the author's competence as a biblical scholar and deems him incompetent theologically to touch on the problem.[167] Joyce more reasonably, although not convincingly, interprets these remarks as referring merely to a permanent separation rather than divorce.[168] The writers who mention the exception clause usually indicate how they interpret the clause. As has already been stated, some of the writers were apparently opposed to the idea that it gives the right of remarriage. The remainder leave the matter clouded in doubt. It is not, however, as Arendzen[169] maintains, evidence which points toward the impossibility of marriage for the innocent party.

Other Reasons.—The only indication in the Ante-Nicene literature that divorce was possible for grounds other than the exception clause comes from Origen. In his

Commentary on the Gospel of Matthew, he discusses the possibility of a valid divorce for such reasons as witchcraft and murder, although apparently he does not accept this lax view. He does, however, suggest that some in the church went beyond the "exception" of the Gospel.

> But now contrary to what was written, some even of the rulers of the church have permitted a woman to marry, even when her husband was living, doing contrary to what was written, where it is said, "A wife is bound for so long time as her husband liveth," and "So then if while her husband liveth, she shall be joined to another man she shall be called an adulteress," not indeed altogether without reason, for it is probable this concession was permitted in comparison with worse things, contrary to what was from the beginning ordained by law, and written.[170]

It is clear that this lax view was contrary to the literal understanding of the New Testament as Origen saw it, but there can be no denying that some churches permitted divorce for other grounds than what was "written." And this was wide-spread enough to be worthy of Origen's comment.

Meaning of "Fornication"

In the Ante-Nicene Church the word for "fornication" (πορνεία) in the exception clause was employed in the general sense that it was used in the period before Jesus and in the New Testament period itself. It is equated at times with "adultery." Hermas, in a passage discussed, counsels a husband to give an unfaithful wife the opportunity to repent, but if she continues to sin, to divorce her but remain unmarried.[171] The Greek word μοιχεία, "adultery," is used twice to describe her action, but if she persists in her unfaithfulness (πορνεία), she is to be divorced. "Fornication" (πορνεία) is also employed to describe the actions of a married person by Tatian[172] and Origen.[173] Sexual offenses in general are classified as "fornication." Justin Martyr uses it as the equivalent of sodomy.[174] A significant insight into the meaning of the word comes by looking at the patristic writers who employed Latin. They changed πορνεία to the Latin word *adulterium*. Thus it is used by Lactantius,[175] Tertullian,[176] and by Cyprian.[177] The word πορνεία could, of course, mean simply "fornication" in the sense of premarital relations. It could be used as a generic term for sexual vice in general. It could be used as a synonym for adultery. There is no evidence in the Ante-Nicene Fathers in contexts dealing with divorce that they ever understood it in any sense other than adultery.

Attitude Toward Candidates for Baptism

Another problem which remains to be commented on is the Ante-Nicene Church's attitude toward pagans who had been married, divorced, and remarried and who desired to become Christians. The crux of the problem is found in the canons of the Synod of Elvira. A relevant passage is:

> If a woman who has been divorced by a catechumen has been married to another husband, she may nevertheless be admitted to baptism. The same rule is to be followed as regards female catechumens.[178]

This would indicate that should a catechumen divorce his wife and she remarry she is to be accepted for baptism. That is, the church here accepts a person who had been divorced and remarried as a valid candidate for baptism. The following canon deals with the discipline that is to be placed on those who marry individuals they know to be illegally divorced. A Christian who married such a man was to receive communion only on her death bed. If a catechumen married such an individual, her baptism was to be postponed for five years, unless she became gravely ill.[179] These two canons from the Synod of Elvira, not noted for its laxity, certainly imply that there was a difference in the rigorous attitude toward sexual conduct applied to those who were already Christians as contrasted with those not yet baptized. There was, as Watkins has shown, a problem in the Ante-Nicene Church pertaining to catechumens.[180] Although they moved in Christian circles, they often postponed baptism as long as possible. Although they were technically not Christians, their conduct could bring disrepute upon the church. Accordingly, there was a tendency to apply Christian ethics to them on the part of the church. In the Ante-Nicene Church, as is indicated by the Synod of Elvira, this disciplinary trend was only beginning to be exerted. There is no question that the marriage of non-Christians was held to be soluble.

The Pauline Privilege is mentioned only by Tertullian among the Ante-Nicene writers. He is more interested in proving that the passage from First Corinthians does not permit a Christian to marry a pagan, than he is with the dissolution of the marriage.[181] He does, however, specifically refer to the fact that the Christian should live with the non-Christian spouse because "we are called in peace" and "as each is called by the Lord, so let him persevere." Both of these principles would have the effect of telling a man who has been divorced himself, or is married to one who has been divorced, to maintain the circumstance in which he was when he became a Christian. If the period following the Council of Nicea be regarded as indicative of the situation which prevailed before the Council, a more complete picture can be drawn. Ambrose taught that marriages among pagans were not indissoluble.[182] Augustine, however, considered remarriage of those separated under the Pauline Privilege to be impossible.[183] The unknown author of the commentary on Paul's epistles, called *The Ambrosiaster*, leaves no doubt that he feels the bond of matrimony was broken by the Privilege and the right to remarry granted.[184] John Chrysostom of Antioch, as a representative of the East, indicates that the Privilege meant a complete severance of the marriage bond, although he does not specifically mention remarriage.[185] This evidence would indicate that despite Augustine's testimony there was a widespread tendency to interpret the Pauline Privilege as breaking the bond of matrimony—a breaking which would rightfully carry with it the possibility of remarriage. The very existence of the Pauline Privilege in this sense at a time when the church did not normally permit Christians to divorce, seems to suggest that the church made a distinction between the marriage of Christians and the marriage of pagans before they presented themselves for baptism. It was not until Augustine that baptism was forbidden remarried catechumens.[186]

SEXUAL MORALITY

The authors of the Ante-Nicene period were prolific in their comments on the subject of sexual morality. Their remarks fell into two categories: first, their criticism of pagan morality which existed about them and their contrast of it with Christian conduct (these passages by the nature of the case are apologetic in tone); secondly, their continual exhortations for their fellow Christians to rise above the common morality of their environment (these references are dialectical and exhortatory in nature).

Early Christian Morality

The patristic writers frequently contrasted the Christian code of conduct with that of their pagan neighbors.

This response on their part was in part solicited by the charges pagans brought against Christianity, especially the accusation that the secret meetings were immoral in nature, not that these charges had grounds in reality. They were largely based on superstition and ignorance of the new movement. Consequently the Fathers answered these charges by maintaining that the pagans were guilty of the very crimes of which they accused the Christians. In making this reply, the Fathers were always careful to point out the higher ideals of Christianity. Justin Martyr insisted that the Christians had an added incentive to right conduct since they believed in a future judgment which would be based on the kind of life they had lived. He further pointed out that it was impossible for them to hide their evil actions from God's detection as men often hide their wrongs from human observation.[187] The method of defense, as previously stated, was to show that the pagans practiced what the pagans condemned. Having quoted the proverb, "The harlot reproves the chaste," Athenagoras rebuked the pagans for reviling "us for the very things which they are conscious of themselves, and ascribe to their own gods, boasting of them as noble deeds, and worthy of the gods."[188] It is they, he continues, "who have set up a market place for fornication, and established infamous resorts for the young for every kind of vile pleasure . . ."[189] In much the same way Minucius Felix replies to the charge that Christians participated in incestuous banquets. He replies that judging from their literature, pagans not only practiced incest themselves, but also worshipped incestuous gods.[190] Tertullian's dry remark on the same subject was that if Christians were guilty of incest, at least they had the sense of conscience to commit it in the darkness and in secret, while the pagans engaged in incestuous practices in the daylight and with full liberty.[191] In connection with incest, a popular charge employed by the Fathers was that through the lax moral situation in society, it was possible to commit incest with one's own offspring without knowing it. This occurs, although in different words, in Minucius Felix,[192] Tertullian,[193] and Clement of Alexandria.[194] When pagans exposed the children of promiscuous relations, so the argument runs, they are often raised for the purpose of prostitution or sodomy. The father, therefore, at some later time can have relations with his own child. Although this sounds rather hypothetical, Tertullian did cite one such case that was publicly known and judged by the Prefect Fuscianus.[195]

The patristic writers were even more outspoken against the practice of sodomy. Justin lamented children being raised for this purpose much as cattle were raised.[196] Athenagoras referred to the markets of homosexuality maintained in the world.[197] Tatian complained that the Romans collected "herds of boys like grazing horses."[198] Tertullian insisted that Christians were heterosexual.[199] The practice of sodomy also comes under condemnation in the Christian portion of the *Sibylline Oracles*.[200] It was, as in many other instances, Clement of Alexandria who gave the fullest exposition. He referred to the young boys in the slave trade,[201] and stated that the Christian answer was to treat every boy as if he were a son.[202] In condemning sodomy, Clement takes the hare as a frequent example in the animal world and reasons that this was the reason the hare was prohibited as meat for the Jews. Moses, he felt, used the hare as a figure for pederasty because of the animal's unnatural sex habits.[203] He also finds the practice of sodomy condemned in the evaluation Paul gives the Gentile world in the opening chapter of Romans. His position is clearly set forth in the following words:

> . . . we must condemn sodomy, all fruitless sowing of seed, and unnatural methods of holding intercourse and the reversal of the sexual role in intercourse.[204]

Having established his position from the Bible, Clement also appeals to philosophy and the ancient Roman law against vice, although he admits that the latter was successfully circumvented by perverts.[205]

Another civil consequence of the promiscuous sex relations, involving a complete disregard for the sanctity of human life, was the practice of infanticide and abortion. When the pagans accused Christians of cannibalism in the Lord's Supper, the non-believers cited the practice of the Christians rescuing the infants abandoned on the dung heaps to give credulence to their charge. In reply, the apologists pointed out the contrast between the Christian attitude toward children and that of the contemporary pagan society. The condition of the world is reflected by Minucius Felix in these words:

> And I see that you at one time expose your begotten children to wild beasts and to birds; at another, that you crush them when strangled with a miserable kind of death. There are some women, who, by drinking medical preparations, extinguish the source of the future man in their very bowels, and thus commit a patricide before they bring forth.[206]

Tertullian enumerates the methods by which the people of the world disposed of their unwanted children, such methods as: exposure to cold, wild beasts, and drowning.[207] Athenagoras,[208] Felix,[209] and Clement all speak of abortion through the use of drugs. Clement speaks of "women who resort to some sort of deadly abortion drug to kill not only the embryo but, along with it, all human kindness."[210] In another place in the same work, Clement has a scathing rebuke of wealthy women who "abandon to exposure the children born to them, yet lavish care on their brood of birds."[211] Murder is forbidden to Christians, Tertullian says, and then reminds his readers that both abortion and infanticide are murder.[212] Lactantius, using the same approach, warns of the attitude which considers infanticide as something less than murder. "Therefore, let no one imagine," he writes, "that even this is allowed, to strangle newly born infants, which is the greatest impiety; for God breathed into their souls for life, and not for death.[213]

The writings of the Fathers abound in descriptions of the depravity of pagan life.[214] It is, however, to Clement of Alexandria that we turn for the most vivid picture.

> But, now, debauched living and indulgence in illicit pleasure have gone to such a limit, and every sort of libertinism has become so rife in the cities, that they have become the norm. Women live in brothels, there offering their own bodies for sale to satisfy lustful pleasures, and boys are taught to renounce their own natures and play the role of women. Self-indulgence has turned everything upside down. Over-refinement in comfortable living has put humanity to shame. It seeks everything, it attempts everything, it forces everything, it violates even nature. Men have become the passive mate in sexual relation and women act as men; contrary to nature, women are both wives and husbands. No opening is impenetrable to impurity. Sexual pleasure is made public property common to all the people, and self-indulgence their boon companion. What a pitiful spectacle! What unspeakable practices! They are monuments to your widespread lack of control, and whores are the proof of your deeds. Alas, such a disregard for law![215]

To leave the impression that the Fathers thought the pagan world entirely void of morality is, of course, false. Clement who presents some of the sharpest criticism of the morality of the world, sums up the pagan condition: "You have hated what was better and valued what was worse, having been spectators in deeds of virtue, but actors of vice."[216] To the finer element in paganism, the Christian writers appealed in order both to convict the immoral conduct of other pagans, and to encourage the Christians by the examples of pagans, who, without Christ, lived above reproach. Thus Justin chides the pagans for conduct which even their own Epicurus and the poets condemn.[217] African Fathers even employ the good conduct of pagans as examples to encourage the Christians to improve their lives. Tertullian, when he wanted to encourage his wife and others to remain unmarried after being widowed, appealed to the Pontifex Maximum who was not allowed to remarry, and concluded: "How greatly purity must please God, since even the enemy affects it."[218] In another work the same author, in combating digamy, cites with approval the requirement that the matron of honor at the marriage of virgins, according to the Roman practice, be married only once.[219] He likewise appeals to the requirement that the Flamines, priests of Rome, could not be digamists.[220] The praise of pagan conduct is especially a technique of Clement of Alexandria. He relies upon his knowledge of Greek literature to bolster his case for sex morality, including appeals to Epicurus,[221], Epictetus,[222], Homer,[223] and Plato.[224]

Christian Morality

The Christian writers were anxious not only to prevent immoral deeds on the part of the faithful, but they were also concerned, as were the Jewish rabbis, with avoiding temptations which might lead to such actions. They correctly perceived the relationship between the inner feelings and drives and overt acts. Consequently, great effort was made to fence off, in good Jewish tradition, the moral laws of Christianity. Great stress was placed on the danger of looking with evil intentions as Jesus linked the two in the adultery of the eye in the Sermon on the Mount. The author of the *Didache* warns Christians against lust, "for lust leads to fornication."[225] In the same passage concern is expressed over the lifting up of the eyes which engenders adultery. Athenagoras quotes the words of Jesus in answering the false charges against Christianity and says, "But we are so far from practicing promiscuous intercourse, that it is not lawful among us to indulge in a lustful look."[226] Tertullian says that in the matter of lusting, Christians are blind.[227] Lustful looking is also condemned by Theophilus,[228] and Clement of Alexandria.[229] On the same level with lust of the eyes, suggestive pictures,[230] immoral poetry,[231] questionable professions, such as acting,[232] banqueting and drinking,[233] mixed bathing or bathing made before slaves,[234] were prohibited to Christians. Even such a religious act as the "holy kiss" was limited to one embrace as a safeguard against temptation.[235] The course of action to be followed in all such circumstances, at least according to Hermas, is for the tempted person to remember his wife, although this is no help for the unmarried.[236] By whatever means temptations were denied, Minucius Felix deemed it so successful that Christians were so innocent that the mere social mingling of the sexes caused them to blush.[237]

The patristic safeguards against temptation were deemed highly successful in controlling extra-marital sexual relations among Christians. Justin, in his *Apology*, denies that Christians are promiscuous.[238] In this affirmation of Christian marital fidelity he is joined by Tatian,[239] Tertullian,[240] and Eusebius.[241] Seduction is not practiced by the disciples of Jesus,[242] writes Tertullian, who adds that marriage is the only sphere of sex activity for them.[243] While these authors make generalizations, Clement of Alexandria is enough of a realist to recognize that being a Christian does not automatically make one immune to temptation. He weaves together Old Testament passages to warn against the evils of fornication.[244] The consequence of fornication, he says, is that the Christian sins against his neighbor and himself; he loses his self-respect which opens the door for immorality. The result of immorality is spiritual death and abandonment by the Word.[245]

Post-marital sins are equally condemned by the Fathers. Ignatius states emphatically that those "who corrupt families shall not inherit the kingdom of God."[246] Almost every author who takes occasion to discuss Christian ethics, speak against adultery. Minucius Felix says that a Christian man has relations with his wife or else he abstains.[247] In this affirmation he is joined by the author of *II Clement*[248] and *Hermas*.[249] It was, as usual

Clement of Alexandria who was most explicit on this subject. His arguments run from the allegorical to the ethical. In one place[250] he employs the hyena, an animal with an insatiable appetite for sex, as a symbol for adultery. The evil of adultery is indicated by the Old Testament prohibition against eating hyena flesh.[251] He seems to be on more solid ground later in the same passage when he suggests the rule that Christians should realize that other men's wives deserve to be treated as though they were daughters.[252]

That commendable morality was not an exclusive possession of Christians was recognized by the Fathers. Indeed, it was Celsus who, in his criticism of Christianity, was quick to point out that Christian morality was no different from that of the philosophers.[253] The Christians' explanation of this fact took different courses. Origen, in his reply to Celsus, attributes the common moral ideals shared by Christians and pagans to God's natural revelation.[254] Clement of Alexandria, on the other hand, taught that the similarity rested in Plato, receiving his position directly from Moses.[255] Whatever the means, the ultimate source of pagan ethics was the Christian's God. Even if pagans and Christians shared a moral ideal, there was considerable difference between a morality as a philosophical idea and morality as a daily approach to life. Christianity, as Origen reminded Celsus, actually transformed a man's conduct. He describes this as meaning:

> . . . from the time they adopt it, (they) have become in some way meeker, and more religious and more consistent, so that certain among them, from desire of exceeding chastity, and from a wish to worship God with greater purity, abstain even from the permitted indulgences of (lawful) love.[256]

The situation was viewed by Methodius as a choice confronting every man. There is an inner struggle between vice and virtue; it is the Christian's task to choose the nobler one.[257] If Christian morality were only a charge to be good, then it would not basically be different from the morality of the philosophers. Christianity not only demands a moral life, it also provides the power for moral living—the Holy Spirit. Thus Clement of Alexandria writes:

> . . . for we are they who bear about with us, in the living and moving image of our human nature, the likeness of God,—a likeness which dwells with us, takes counsel with us, feels with us, feels for us. We have become a consecrated offering to God for Christ's sake; we are a chosen generation, the royal priesthood, the holy nation, the peculiar people . . . who have learned to walk in newness of life.[258]

Despite the church's teaching on purity and the power of the Spirit, it was inevitable that some would fall short of the desired conduct. The repetitious exhortations of the Fathers to moral living themselves suggest that temptations were great and that many succumbed. Hermas mentions Christians who wandered away and "walked in the lusts and deceits of the world."[259] Tertullian is more specific and lists fornication,[260] adultery, and abortion[261] among the professed followers of Christ. In fact, the North African advises the young not to be baptized until married as the means of protecting Christian purity.[262] There is, of course, no way of ascertaining the degree of immorality in the Ante-Nicene Church. Because Christian morality was high and demanding, any shortcoming became glaring. The references to immoral conduct, therefore, need not suggest widespread laxity. To recognize that Christians fell below the ideal, or to admit that pagans reached the ideal, in no way distorts the fact that the moral tone of the followers of Jesus was far above the common morality of their environment.

CONCLUSIONS

Marriage was held by the Ante-Nicene Church to be a part of God's plan. Such unions were monogamous in nature and for the specific purpose of procreation. This cooperation with the Creator was expressed in the religious aura which soon became attached to matrimony. While marriage was not yet held to be a sacrament, the sacramental seed was germinating in the church by this time. It developed, in part, by attributing to God various secular functions and ceremonies related to marriage as they existed in the Roman society. At the same time this exaltation of marriage was taking place, there was also a growing tendency to depreciate the married state. Philosophical, theological, and ethical factors combined to produce this tendency which found expression in attempts to limit sexual relations in marriage to the conceiving of children, to promote celibacy as a higher spiritual state, and finally to condemn certain unions. Mixed marriages between Christians and non-Christians and digamous unions, or the remarriage after the death of the first mate, were expressly forbidden by some. Tertullian makes a significant concession in that he permitted the remarriage of individuals if they were widowed before they became Christians.

Christians, like others in the Hellenistic world, always possessed the legal right of divorce. Although they had the legal right to do so, not all believed they had the religious right. Some believed, in fact, that a Christian should not divorce a mate regardless of the grounds. Among the authors of this period, Hermas, Tertullian, and Clement of Alexandria made statements which might uphold this position. Tertullian and Clement's statements are ambiguous and can be interpreted as if they assumed, although they did not state, the right to divorce under certain conditions. At any rate, these two authors elsewhere make statements indicating they accepted the right to divorce on the grounds of adultery. All three of these men mention, in the context where they seemingly deny the right of divorce, the possibility of the reconciliation of the couple. Thus their attitude toward divorce and remarriage may have been shaped by the hope of such a reconciliation. The Synods of Elvira and Arles adopted canons which likewise can be interpreted as prohibiting divorce. The former Synod prohibited the innocent partner of an adulterous mate, if subsequently remarried, from receiving communion unless gravely ill. This need not be taken, however, as a denial of the right to divorce. In divorces which did not involve an adulterous relation, the remarried Christian was not to receive communion even at death. Divorce on the grounds of adultery, hence, was judged differently than other divorces. The Synod of Arles considered the innocent party in an adulterous relationship under an obligation not to remarry. But it anticipated that the innocent might remarry and advised "strong counsel" against such action. It did not, however, instruct any form of excommunication for those who ignored the counsel. As was suggested above, the attitude toward divorce and remarriage in the Ante-Nicene Church was influenced by the belief concerning repentance. It was generally held, until the close of the third century, that there was only one opportunity for repentance after baptism. Further, it was accepted that adultery, along with idolatry and murder, was a sin which was not within the church's power to forgive, but could only be forgiven by God on the Day of Judgment. A necessary corollary of this doctrine was a strict view toward every situation which involved adultery or potentially involved adultery. It is thus significant that when the church's attitude about repentance changed, its rigorism concerning divorce and remarriage was relaxed. Dionysius, Hermas, Clement of Alexandria, and Callistus all believed that adultery was within the church's prerogative of forgiveness. Gradually this position gained popularity until finally systems of graded penance, which included the sin of adultery, were adopted by the synods.

Some writers discuss the matter of divorce without mentioning the exception clause. This does not mean, however, that they denied the possibility of divorce. Among this number are Justin, Athenagoras, and Cyprian. There is the possibility that Justin assumes, although he does not mention, the clause. Athenagoras quotes from the Gospel of Mark where there is no exception clause so there is no significance attached to its absence. Cyprian quotes from I Corinthians 7, and there is no importance placed on the clause being absent from his remarks since it is not in Paul's letter. The exception clause is mentioned by Theophilus, Clement of Alexandria, Origen, Tertullian, and Lactantius. Although some of these writers deny the right of remarriage, they are clear about the right of divorce on grounds of adultery. Since Origen only suggests the possibility of divorce for reasons other than adultery and the passages which seem to suggest the impossibility of divorce can be explained on other grounds, the common position of the Ante-Nicene Church was to allow divorce on grounds of adultery. The word "adultery" was used by the Fathers, as by the biblical writers, for all illegal sexual relations. Most often, however, the word was employed to mean post-marital sexual relations.

The evidence concerning the church's attitude toward divorced pagans who presented themselves for baptism is scant. The material available does indicate that a distinction was made between people who were divorced and remarried before they became Christians and those who did so after their conversion. The canons of the Synod of Elvira suggest that a catechumen who had been divorced and remarried could still receive Christian baptism. The same Synod also considered the case of one who married a person known to be illegally divorced. If the person who is so united is a Christian, he is to be denied communion unless he is near death. If the person is only a catechumen, he is required to postpone his baptism for five additional years. The distinction between Christians and non-Christians is also seen in Tertullian's permitting a digamous union for those widowed before baptism. There is no suggestion that the person was required to leave an illegally divorced spouse. Tertullian, who is the only author in the period under consideration to mention the Pauline Privilege, indicates that Christians were to remain in whatever state they were called.

The writers of this period provide detailed criticism of the moral tone of non-Christian society. Prodded in part by their natural abhorrence of the situation and in part by the need to defend Christianity against pagan charges of immorality, they were outspoken against extramarital relations. Especially offensive were those acts which in their minds depreciated or perverted God's creation, namely: homosexuality, infanticide, and abortion. The abhorrence with which the Fathers viewed the pagan scene did not blind them to the virtue which did exist in the world. To this they appealed as an encouragement for better living on the part of pagans and Christians alike. Among themselves the Christians took precaution against immoral conduct. They viewed the ethics of the New Testament not as a high ideal, but as a necessary reality possible of realization through the Holy Spirit. Christianity required and received a more demanding moral conduct than that which prevailed in the society in which the Christians lived.

Chapter V Footnotes

[1]*Chastity,* ix.
[2]*Stromata,* ii. 23.
[3]*Monogamy,* x.
[4]A. Esmein, *Le mariage en Droit Canonique* (Paris: 1912), I, 106.
[5]*Shepherd of Hermas,* Vis. iv. 2.
[6]*I Clement,* xxxii. 5-6.
[7]*Epistle to Diognetus,* v. 6.
[8]*I Apology,* xxix. 1.
[9]*Dialogue with Trypho,* cx.
[10]*Plea for Christians,* xxxiii.
[11]*Treatise on the Soul,* xxvii.
[12]*Ibid.*
[13]*Banquet of the Ten Virgins,* ii. 1.
[14]*Theophilus to Autoclycus,* ii. 28.
[15]*Against Marcion,* i. 29.
[16]*Stromata,* iii. 3.13.
[17]*Stromata,* iii. 12.84.
[18]Socrates, *Ecclesiastical History,* i. 11.
[19]Tertullian calls it a sacrament, but he could not have meant the doctrinal teaching of a later time. *Chastity,* v.
[20]*Epistle to Polycarp,* v.
[21]*To His Wife,* ii. 8.
[22]Nepos, *Atticus,* xii. 2.
[23]*To His Wife, op. cit.,* ii. 8.
[24]*Ibid.*
[25]*Commentary on Matthew,* xiv. 16.
[26]*Stromata,* iv. 20.
[27]*Educator,* iii. 11.63.
[28]Joyce, *op. cit.,* p. 215.
[29]W. M. Foley, "Marriage (Christian)," *Encyclopedia of Religion and Ethics,* ed. James Hasting (New York: Charles Scribner's Sons, 1922), VIII, p. 435.
[30]*Ibid.,* p. 433.
[31]*Educator,* iii. 6.34; iii. 12.92.
[32]*On Purity,* xvi.

[33]*Dialogue with Trypho,* cx.
[34]*Ibid.,* cxxxiv.
[35]*Theophilus to Autolycus,* ii. 28.
[36]*Against Celsus,* viii. 55.
[37]*Plea for Christians,* xxxiii.
[38]*Stromata,* iii. 12.82.
[39]*Monogamy,* ix.
[40]*Supra,* pp. 55-56.
[41]*To His Wife,* i. 2.
[42]*Apology,* xlvi.
[43]*Banquet of the Ten Virgins,* i. 2.
[44]*Institutes,* iii. 22.
[45]Ireneaus, *Heresies,* i. 5.3.; i. 13; Clement, *Stromata,* iii. 4; Eusebius, *Ecclesiastical History,* iv. 7.9.
[46]André Falloux, "Platonisme des Pères," *Dictionnaire de Théologie Catholique,* XII, 2 Partie, 2390.
[47]Pierre Pouratt, *Christian Spiritualism* (Westminster, Maryland: The Newman Press, 1953), I, p. 67.
[48]Henry Chadwick, *Alexandrian Christianity* (Philadelphia: The Westminster Press, 1952), p. 36.
[49]Max Thurian, *Mariage et Célibat* (Paris: Delachaux et Niestlé, 1955), p. 20.
[50]*Plea for Christians,* xxxiii.
[51]*I Apology,* xxix. 1.
[52]*Educator,* ii. 10.102.
[53]*Ibid.,* 91.
[54]Sherwin Bailey, *Sexual Relations in Christian Thought* (New York: Harper and Brothers, 1959), p. 214 ff.
[55]*I Clement,* xxxviii. 2.
[56]*Polycarp,* v. 2-3.
[57]*Plea for Christians,* xxxiii.
[58]*Apology,* ix.
[59]*Monogamy,* viii.
[60]*Commentaria ad Romanos,* ix. 1.
[61]*Homiliae in Numeros,* vi.
[62]*To His Wife,* i. 3.
[63]*Ibid.,* 5.
[64]Fagley, *op. cit.,* p. 157.

[65]*On Purity*, xvi.
[66]*On the Dress of Virgins*, xxiii.
[67]*Banquet of the Ten Virgins*, i. 2.
[68]*Ibid.*, 11.
[69]*Ibid.*, 8.
[70]*I Clement*, xxxviii. 2.
[71]*Stromata*, iii. 1.4.
[72]*I Apology*, xxix. 2-3.
[73]Eusebius, *op. cit.*, v. 28.5.
[74]*Educator*, iii. 4.26.
[75]Herbert Thurston, "Celibacy," *Catholic Encyclopedia*, ed. Charles Herberman (New York: Universal Knowledge Foundation, 1937), III, 487.
[76]H. Achelis, "Agapetae," *Encyclopedia of Religion and Ethics*, I. 273.
[77]*Chastity*, vii. 9.
[78]Socrates, *Ecclesiastical History*, i. 11.
[79]*Visions*, ii. 2.3.
[80]*Similitudes*, ix. 11.3.
[81]*Chastity*, xii.
[82]*Monogamy*, xvi.
[83]*Heresies*, i. 6.3.
[84]*Epistle*, lxi.
[85]Eusebius, *op. cit.*, vii. 30.
[86]Ireneaus, *Heresies*, i. 6.3.
[87]Eusebius, *op. cit.*, v. 15.
[88]Tertullian, *The Prescription of Heresies*, xxx.
[89]*Epistle*, lxi.
[90]Canon xxvii.
[91]Canon xix.
[92]Canon iii.
[93]*Supra*, p. 16.
[94]*Mandates*, iv.
[95]*I Apology*, xv.
[96]*Plea for Christians*, xxiii.
[97]Herbert Preisker, *op. cit.*, p. 194.
[98]*Chastity*, xi.
[99]*To His Wife*, i. 4.

[100]*Apology*, vi. 6.
[101]*To His Wife*, i. 8.
[102]*Stromata*, iii. 1.4.
[103]*Homiliae in Lucam*, xvii.
[104]*Refutation of All Heresies*, ix. 7.
[105]Herbert Preisker, *op. cit.*, p. 242 f.
[106]*To His Wife*, ii. 3.
[107]*Ibid.*, 7.
[108]*Testimonies*, iii. 62.
[109]*To His Wife*, ii. 2.
[110]Hippolytus, *Refutation of All Heresies*, ix. 7.
[111]L. ix. Dig. 24.2.
[112]L. vii. Cod. 5.17.
[113]*On the Manner in Which the Persecutors Died*, xiii.
[114]*De Non Iterando Conjugio*, li.
[115]*Expositio Evangelii Secundum Lucam*, viii.
[116]*Mandates*, iv. 1.6.
[117]*Ibid.*, 1.8.
[118]*Monogamy*, ix.
[119]*Patience*, xii.
[120]*To His Wife*, ii. 3.
[121]*Stromata*, ii. 23.
[122]*Ibid.*
[123]*Mandates*, iv. 1.8.
[124]*Patience*, xii.
[125]*Stromata*, ii. 23.
[126]*Against Marcion*, iv. 34.
[127]Joyce, *op. cit.*, p. 308.
[128]Luckock, *op. cit.*, p. 115.
[129]*Stromata*, iii. 6.50.
[130]Charles J. Hefele, *A History of the Christian Councils*, trans. Wm. R. Clark (Edinburgh: T. and T. Clark, 1871), I, p. 137.
[131]Canon viii.
[132]Canon ix.
[133]Hefele, *op. cit.*, p. 130.
[134]Canon x.
[135]Tertullian, *On Purity*, v.; Origen, *On Prayer*, xxviii. 10.
[136]*On Purity*, xviii.

[137]*On Penitence,* vii.

[138]O. D. Watkins, *A History of Penance* (London: Longmans, Green and Co., 1920), I, 72.

[139]*Against Heresies,* i. 13.

[140]Eusebius, *op. cit.*, iv. 23.

[141]*Stromata,* ii. 23.

[142]*Refutation of All Heresies,* ix. 7.

[143]*On Purity,* i.

[144]*Ibid.*, xxii.

[145]Roland H. Bainton, *What Christianity Says About Sex, Love and Marriage* (New York: Association Press, 1957), p. 35.

[146]*Canonical Epistle,* i.

[147]Canon xvi.

[148]Canon i.

[149]Canon iii.

[150]Hefele, *op. cit.*, p. 225.

[151]Canon vii.

[152]Canon xlvii.

[153]Canon lxix.

[154]Canon lxxviii.

[155]Canon lxxii.

[156]Canon xxi.

[157]*I Apology,* xv.

[158]*Plea for Christians,* xxxiii.

[159]*Testimonies,* iii. 90.

[160]Harold Smith, "Our Lord's Teaching on Divorce," *Expositor,* XVI (November, 1919), p. 361.

[161]*Theophilus to Autolycus,* iii. 13.

[162]*Stromata,* ii. 23.

[163]*Commentary on Matthew,* xiv. 16.

[164]*Monogamy,* ix.

[165]*Institute,* vi. 23.

[166]*Epitome of the Institutes,* lxvi.

[167]Luckock, *op. cit.*, p. 138.

[168]Joyce, *op. cit.*, p. 309.

[169]J. P. Arendzen, "Ante-Nicene Interpretations of the Sayings on Divorce," *The Journal of Theological Studies,* XX (1919), p. 241.

[170]*Commentary on Matthew*, xiv. 23.
[171]*Mandates*, iv. 1.5.
[172]*Oration to the Greeks*, x.
[173]*Commentary on Matthew*, xiv. 17.
[174]*I Apology*, i. 27.
[175]*Institutes*, vi. 23.
[176]*Against Marcion*, iv. 34.
[177]*The Good of Patience*, vi.
[178]Canon x.
[179]Canon xi.
[180]O. D. Watkins, *Holy Matrimony, op. cit.*, p. 465.
[181]*To His Wife*, ii. 2.
[182]*Commentaria Epistolam B. Pauli and Corinthios Primam*, vii. 12.
[183]*To Pollintius on Adulterous Marriage*, i. 18.
[184]*I Corinthians*, vii.
[185]*I Corinthians Homily*, xix.
[186]*Faith and Works*, i. 2.
[187]*I Apology*, xii.
[188]*Plea for Christians*, xxxiv.
[189]*Ibid.*
[190]*Octavius*, xxxi.
[191]*To the Nations*, i. 16.
[192]*Octavius*, xxxi.
[193]*Apology*, ix.
[194]*Educator*, iii. 3.21.
[195]*To the Nations*, i. 16.
[196]*I Apology*, xxvii.
[197]*Plea for Christians*, xxxiv.
[198]*Oration to the Greeks*, xxviii.
[199]*Apology*, xlvi.
[200]*Sibylline Oracles*, v. 165-167.
[201]*Educator*, iii. 3.21.
[202]*Ibid.*, ii. 10.90.
[203]*Ibid.*, 10.83.
[204]*Educator*, ii. 10.87.
[205]*Ibid.*, iii. 3.22.
[206]*Octavius*, xxx.

[207]*To the Nations,* i. 15.
[208]*Plea for Christians,* xxxv.
[209]*Octavius,* xxx.
[210]*Educator,* ii. 10.96.
[211]*Ibid.,* iii. 4.30.
[212]*Apology,* ix.
[213]*Institutes,* vi. 20.
[214]Tertullian, *To the Nations,* i. 16; *Theophilus to Autolycus,* i. 2; Justin, *Dialogue with Trypho,* iv. 3; Origen, *Against Celsus,* ii. 79.
[215]*Educator,* iii. 3.21.
[216]*Exhortation to the Greeks,* iv.
[217]*II Apology,* xii.
[218]*To His Wife,* i. 7.
[219]*Chastity,* xiii.
[220]H. J. Rose, "Flamines," *The Oxford Classical Dictionary* (Oxford: Clarendon Press, 1949), p. 364.
[221]*Exhortation to the Greeks,* ii.
[222]*Ibid.,* viii.
[223]*Stromata,* iii. 3.14.
[224]*Ibid.,* 17.
[225]*Didache,* iii. 3.
[226]*Plea for Christians,* xxxii.
[227]*Apology,* xlvi.
[228]*Theophilus to Autolycus,* iii. 3.
[229]*Educator,* iii. 11.69-70.
[230]*Exhortation to the Greeks,* iv.
[231]*Plea for Christians,* xxi.
[232]Cyprian, *Epistle,* lx.
[233]*Educator,* ii. 7.54.
[234]*Ibid.,* iii. 5.31.
[235]*Plea for Christians,* xxxii.
[236]*Mandates,* iv. 1.
[237]*Octavius,* xxxi.
[238]*I Apology,* xix.
[239]*Oration to the Greeks,* xxxiii.
[240]*Chastity,* ix.
[241]Eusebius, *op. cit.,* viii. 12.

[242]*Apology,* xliv.
[243]*Chastity,* iv.
[244]*Educator,* ii. 10.101.
[245]*Ibid.,* 10.100.
[246]*Polycarp,* xvi.
[247]*Octavius,* xxxi.
[248]*II Clement,* iv. 3; vi. 4.
[249]*Mandates,* iv. 1.
[250]*Educator,* iii. 10.83.
[251]*Deut.,* 14:7.
[252]*Educator,* iii. 10.90.
[253]*Against Celsus,* i. 4.
[254]*Ibid.*
[255]*Educator,* iii. 10.90-91.
[256]*Against Celsus,* i. 26.
[257]*Banquet of the Ten Virgins,* xvii.
[258]*Exhortation to the Greeks,* iv.
[259]*Visions,* vi. 3.3.
[260]*On Purity,* ix.
[261]*Concerning the Veiling of Virgins,* xiv.
[262]*On Baptism,* xviii.

CHAPTER VI

SUMMARY AND CONCLUSIONS

After completing the study of the attitude of the Ante-Nicene Church toward the divorce and remarriage of Christians and catechumens, a conclusion with a resume of the findings is in order.

SUMMARY

Marriage was held in honor in the society in which Christianity moved, whether Jewish or Hellenistic. Toward the close of the period investigated, there was a tendency in the Gentile world to depreciate marriage, which had an effect on the birth rate and became the subject of imperial legislation. Although many factors contributed to this view of marriage, an ascetic spirit was prominent as a determining factor. Departing from its Jewish heritage, the church was influenced by this spirit especially in the exaltation of celibacy, not as an expediency, as in the New Testament Church, but as a higher walk of life. Marriage among the Gentiles as well as the

Christians was monogamous in nature, and for practical purposes this was also the form in Judaism, although polygamy was permissible both by doctrine and by concession of the Roman law.

Divorce was common among both the Jews and Gentiles, the grounds upon which it was obtainable being rather liberal. In Hellenistic society either mate could secure a divorce, or it was possible to dissolve the union, of course, through mutual consent. In Judaism only the husband technically had the right of divorce, but the woman by the time of the Common Era was not left without recourse. The terminology of the Jewish process, with the husband "divorcing" and the wife "leaving," continued to persist and shaped Christian statements of the subject. The Christian attitude toward divorce was two-fold. No other explanation is as free of difficulties as to admit that in the Ante-Nicene Church there were both rigorists and liberals in regard to the possibility of divorce. The Church Fathers certainly accepted the Matthean exception clauses. The rigorists' position concerning the indissolubility of marriage gained an impetus from the church's: (a) abhorrence of the moral indifference of Gentile society, as is indicated by the Fathers' extreme position in regard to the social mixing of the sexes: (b) withdrawal from all aspects of society that might tend to weaken the moral fiber of the church; and (c) limiting of sexual intercourse to the purpose of procreation. Remarriage was also discouraged by the doctrine of penance in the Ante-Nicene Church. First, adultery was viewed among the rigorists to be beyond the Church's prerogative to forgive. Forgiveness was not impossible but could only be done at the Last Judgment of God. Secondly, the attitude was influenced by the doctrine that there was only one repentance for post-baptismal sins. Individuals would not be encouraged to remarry lest they make reconciliation impossible. The Pauline Privilege indicates a distinction was made as to the permanency in a mixed union as contrasted with a marriage in which both parties were Christians. A similar distinction was made by the Council of Elvira. This is based on the fact that non-Christians were not held responsible for the Christian doctrine of marriage and divorce.

The sexual morals in Judaism were high, and the rabbis sought for continued purity in safeguards from temptation. Morality in the Hellenistic world, however, was very low. Christian morals, in contrast to the pagan environment, were elevated and demanding. The severity of Christian ethics was in part a reaction to the false charge of immorality leveled against the church and a genuine abhorrence of the immorality of the pagan world.

CONCLUSIONS

Since both Jewish and Roman society freely permitted divorce, it was impossible for the Ante-Nicene Church to ignore completely the issue of divorce and remarriage. Having briefly summarized the material, it is now possible to state that the evidence supports the following conclusions.

The Ante-Nicene Church permitted divorce on the grounds of unchastity. In response to rigorist tendencies made necessary by paganism, this policy was never denied; it was only redefined. By "divorce" the church came to mean not a complete break of the union with the right of remarriage, but only "separation" from bed and board. In addition, the right to remarry was not in keeping with the theology of only one repentance after baptism, for it would make reconciliation impossible.

The Ante-Nicene Church did not sit in judgment on the pre-Christian morals of the catechumens. That non-Christians were not accountable for Christian ethics is indicated by: the Pauline Privilege which places marriages involving a pagan on a different level than those between Christians; the Pauline concept of natural revelation and the responsibility of the Gentiles; and the Council of Elvira. The subject is mentioned specifically only in the canons of the Council where a distinction is made between the case of a divorced and remarried catechumen and a divorced and remarried Christian. There is nothing to indicate in the literature of the period that a divorced and remarried catechumen was required to make any change in his marital status before being accepted for baptism. The silence on this matter in the Church Fathers is all the more significant since the church for a portion of this period was so influenced by rigorist tendencies that adultery, which consecutive marriages would amount to by the contemporary Christian standards, was so severely judged that it was deemed beyond the prerogative of the church to forgive.

BIBLIOGRAPHY

A. PRIMARY SOURCES

All references to *The Ante-Nicene Fathers* are to the reprint (Grand Rapids, Michigan: Wm. B. Eerdmans Company, 1951) of the American Edition (Buffalo, New York: The Christian Literature Publishing Company, 1885 ff.) of The Ante-Nicene Christian Library (Edinburgh: T. and T. Clark, 1865 ff.).

Ambrosius. *Expositio Evangelii Secundum Lucam.* Tomus XV of *Patrologiae Latinae.* Edited by J. P. Migne. Parisiis, 1887.

—. *Pauli ad Corinthios Primam.* Tomus XVII of *Patrologiae Latinae.* Edited by J. P. Migne. Parisiis, 1879.

Apocrypha and Pseudepigrapha of the Old Testament. Edited by R. H. Charles. Oxford: Clarendon Press, 1913.

Aramaic Papyri of the Fifth Century B. C. Trans. A. Cowley. Oxford: Clarendon Press, 1923.

Athenagoras. *Plea for Christians.* Vol. II of *The Ante-Nicene Fathers.* Trans. B. P. Pratten. 10 vols. Grand Rapids, Michigan: Wm. B. Eerdmans Company, 1951.

Augustine. *Adulterous Marriages.* Vol. XXVII of *Fathers of the Church.* Edited by R. J. Deferrari. Trans. Charles T. Huegelmeyer. New York: Fathers of the Church, Inc., 1955.

—. *Faith and Works*. Vol. XXVII of *Fathers of the Church*. Edited by R. J. Deferrari. Trans. Sister Marie Liguori. New York: Fathers of the Church, Inc., 1955.

Babylonian Talmud. Edited by I. Epstein. 30 vols. London: Soncino Press, 1935-1948.

Canons. In *A History of the Christian Councils*. Edited by Charles Hefele, Trans. Wm. R. Clark *et al.* 5 vols. Edinburgh: T. & T. Clark, 1871-1896.

Capitolinus, Julius. *Marcus Antonius, The Philosopher*. Vol. I of *Scriptores Historia Augusta* in *The Loeb Classical Library*. Trans. David Magie. 3 vols. New York: G. P. Putnam's Sons, 1922-1932.

Chrysostomi. *De non iterando coniugio*. Tomus XLVIII of *Patrologiae Graecae*. Edited by J.P. Migne. Parisiis, 1839.

—. *Homilies on I Corinthians*. Vol. XXVII of *Library of the Fathers of the Holy Catholic Church*. Edited by E. B. Pusey, J. Keble, and J. H. Newman. Trans. J. Ashworth. Oxford: 1848.

Cicero, Marcus Tullius. *Pro Caelio*. In *The Loeb Classical Library*. Trans. R. Gardner. New York: G. P. Putnam's Sons, 1952.

—. *To His Friends*. In *The Loeb Classical Library*. Trans. H. Grace Hodge. 3 vols. New York: G. P. Putnam's Sons, 1927-1929.

Clement of Alexandria. *Christ the Educator*. Vol. XXIII of *Fathers of the Church*. Edited by R. J. Deferrari. Trans. Simon P. Wood. New York: Fathers of the Church, Inc., 1954.

—. *Exhortation to the Greeks.* Vol. II of *The Ante-Nicene Fathers.* Trans. W. Wilson. 10 vols. Grand Rapids, Michigan: Wm. B. Eerdmans Company, 1951.

—. *Stromata.* Vol. II of *The Ante-Nicene Fathers.* Trans. W. Wilson. 10 vols. Grand Rapids, Michigan: Wm. B. Eerdmans Company, 1951.

—. *Stomateis.* Book III in *Alexandrian Christianity.* Vol. II of *The Library of Christian Classics.* Trans. J. E. L. Oulton. Philadelphia: The Westminster Press, 1954.

Clement of Rome. *First Clement.* In *The Apostolic Fathers* in *The Loeb Classical Library.* Trans. Kirsopp Lake. 2 vols. New York: G. P. Putnam's Sons, 1913-1914.

Cyprian. *Epistles.* Vol. I of the *Writings of Cyprian* in the *Ante-Nicene Christian Library.* Trans. Robert Wallis. 3 vols. Edinburgh: T. & T. Clark, 1868.

—. *On the Dress of Virgins.* In *Saint Cyprian Treatises, The Fathers of the Church.* Trans. Sister Angela Elizabeth Keanan. New York: The Fathers of the Church, Inc., 1958.

—. *Testimonies.* Vol. II of the *Writings of Cyprian* in the *Ante-Nicene Christian Library.* Trans. Robert E. Wallis. 3 vols. Edinburgh: T. & T. Clark, 1869.

Demosthenes. *In Neaeram.* Vol. VI in *Demosthenes* in *The Loeb Classical Library.* Trans. A. T. Murray. 7 vols. Cambridge, Massachusetts: Harvard University Press, 1926-1949.

Didaché. In *The Apostolic Fathers* in *The Loeb Classical*

Library. Trans. Kirsopp Lake. 2 vols. New York: G. P. Putnam's Sons, 1913-1914.

Digest of Justinian. Trans. C. H. Monro. 2 vols. Cambridge: University Press, 1904-1909.

Dio Cassius. *Dio's Roman History*. In *The Loeb Classical Library*. Trans. Earnest Cary. 9 vols. New York: The Macmillan Company, 1914-1928.

Diodorus Siculus. *Diodorus of Sicily*. In *The Loeb Classical Library*. Trans. C. H. Oldfather, C. Bradford Welles, Russel M. Geer, and F. R. Walton. 11 vols. New York: G. P. Putnam's Sons, 1933-1958.

Dionysius of Halicarnassus. *Roman Antiquities*. In *The Loeb Classical Library*. Trans. Earnest Cary. 7 vols. Cambridge, Massachusetts: Harvard University Press, 1937-1950.

Epictetus. *Arrian's Discourses, The Manual, and Fragments*. In *The Loeb Classical Library*. Trans. W. A. Oldfather. 2 vols. New York: G. P. Putnam's Sons, 1926-1928.

—. *Encheiridion*. In *Arrian's Discourses, The Manual, and Fragments* in *The Loeb Classical Library*. Trans. W. A. Oldfather. 2 vols. New York: G. P. Putnam's Sons, 1926-1928.

Epistle to Diognetus. Trans. Henry G. Meecham. Manchester: University Press, 1949.

Epitome of the Institutes. Vol. VII of *The Ante-Nicene Fathers*. Trans. William Fletcher. 10 vols. Grand Rapids, Michigan: Wm. B. Eerdmans Company, 1951.

Eusebius Pamphili. *The Ecclesiastical History*. In *The*

Loeb Classical Library. Trans. Kirsopp Lake and J. E. L. Oulston. 2 vols. Cambridge, Massachusetts: Harvard University Press, 1949-1957.

Gaius. *Institutes of Roman Law.* Trans. Edward Poste. Oxford: Clarendon Press, 1914.

Gellius, Aulus. *The Attic Nights of Aulus Gellius.* In *The Loeb Classical Library.* Trans. John C. Rolfe. New York: G. P. Putnam's Sons, 1928.

Gregory Thaumaturgus. *Canonical Epistle.* Vol. VI of *The Ante-Nicene Fathers.* Trans. D. F. Salmond. 10 vols. Grand Rapids, Michigan: Wm. B. Eerdmans Company, 1951.

Hermas. *Shepherd of Hermas.* In *The Apostolic Fathers* in *The Loeb Classical Library.* Trans. Kirsopp Lake. 2 vols. New York: G. P. Putnam's Sons, 1913-1914.

Hippolytus. *Refutation of All Heresies.* Vol. V of *The Ante-Nicene Fathers.* Trans. J. H. Macmahon. 10 vols. Grand Rapids, Michigan: Wm. B. Eerdmans Company, 1951.

Holy Bible. Revised Standard Version. New York: Thomas Nelson & Sons, 1957.

Horatius Flaccus, Quintus. *Satires, Epistles, Ars Poetica.* In *The Loeb Classical Library.* Trans. Thomas Fairclough. New York: G. P. Putnam's Sons, 1926.

Ignatius. *Epistle to Polycarp.* Vol. I of *The Apostolic Fathers* in *The Loeb Classical Library.* Trans. Kirsopp Lake. 2 vols. New York: G. P. Putnam's Sons, 1913-1914.

Ireneaus. *Against Heresies.* Vol. I of *The Ante-Nicene*

Fathers. Trans. A. Cleveland Coxe. 10 vols. Grand Rapids, Michigan: Wm. B. Eerdmans, 1951.

Josephus, Flavius. *Against Apion*. In *The Loeb Classical Library*. Trans. H. Thackeray. New York: G. P. Putnam's Sons, 1926.

—. *Antiquities*. In *The Loeb Classical Library*. Trans. H. Thackeray, Ralph Marcus, and Allen Winkgren. 5 vols. New York: G. P. Putnam's Sons, 1930-1963.

Justin Martyr. *Dialogue with Trypho*. Vol. I of *The Ante-Nicene Fathers*. Trans. A. Cleveland Coxe. 10 vols. Grand Rapids, Michigan: Wm. B. Eerdmans Company, 1951.

—. *First Apology*. Vol. I of *The Ante-Nicene Fathers*. Trans. A. Cleveland Coxe. 10 vols. Grand Rapids, Michigan: Wm. B. Eerdmans Company, 1951.

—. *Second Apology*. Vol. I of *The Ante-Nicene Fathers*. Trans. A. Cleveland Coxe. 10 vols. Grand Rapids, Michigan: Wm. B. Eerdmans Company, 1951.

Juvenal, Decimus Junius. *Satires*. In *The Loeb Classical Library*. Trans. G. G. Ramsay and William Gifford. 2 vols. New York: G. P. Putnam's Sons, 1918.

Lactantius. *The Divine Institutes*. Vol. VII of *The Ante-Nicene Fathers*. Trans. William Fletcher. 10 vols. Grand Rapids, Michigan: Wm. B. Eerdmans Company, 1951.

—. *On the Manner in Which the Persecutors Died*. Vol. VII of *The Ante-Nicene Fathers*. Trans. William Fletcher. 10 vols. Grand Rapids, Michigan: Wm. B. Eerdmans Company, 1951.

Lamprides, Aelius. *Severus Alexander.* Vol. II of *Scriptores Historia Augusta* in *The Loeb Classical Library.* Trans. David Magie. 3 vols. New York: G. P. Putnam's Sons, 1922-1932.

Maimon, Moses ben. *More Nevochim* in *The Reasons of the Laws of Moses.* Trans. James Townley. London: Longman, Rees, Orne, Brown and Green, 1827.

Martialis, Marcus Valerius. *Epigrams.* In *The Loeb Classical Library,* Trans. Walter C. A. Ker. 2 vols. New York: G. P. Putnam's Sons, 1919-1920.

Methodius. *Banquet of the Ten Virgins.* Vol. VI of *The Ante-Nicene Fathers.* Trans. W. H. Clark, 10 vols. Grand Rapids, Michigan: Wm. B. Eerdmans, 1951.

Minucius Felix. *Octavius.* Vol. III of *The Ante-Nicene Fathers.* Trans. Robert E. Wallis. 10 vols. Grand Rapids, Michigan: Wm. B. Eerdmans Company, 1951.

Mishnah. Trans. Herbert Danby. Oxford: Clarendon Press, 1933.

Nepos, Cornelius. *Atticus* in *Lucius Annaeus, Florus and Cornelius Nepos.* In *The Loeb Classical Library.* Trans. J. C. Rolfe. New York: G. P. Putnam's Sons, 1924.

Origen. Against Celsus. Vol. IV of *The Ante-Nicene Fathers.* Trans. Frederick Crombie. 10 vols. Grand Rapids, Michigan: Wm. B. Eerdmans Company, 1951.

—. *Commentaria in Epistolam B. Pavli ad Romanos.* Tomus XIV of *Patrologiae Graecae.* Edited by J. P. Migne. Parisiis, 1856.

—. *Commentary of Matthew.* Vol. X of *The Ante-Nicene Fathers.* Trans. John Patrick. 10 vols. Grand Rapids,

Michigan: Wm. B. Eerdmans Company, 1951.
—. *Homiliae in Lucam*. Tomus XIII of *Petrologiae Graecae*. Edited by J. P. Migne. Parisiis, 1858.
—. *Homiliae in Numeros*. Tomus XII of *Patrologiae Graecae*. Edited by J. P. Migne. Parisiis, 1856.
—. *On Prayer*. In *Alexandrian Christianity*. Vol. II of *The Library of Christian Classics*. Trans. J. E. L. Oulton. Philadelphia: The Westminster Press, 1954.
Ovidius Naso, Publius. *The Art of Love*. In *The Loeb Classical Library*. Trans. J. H. Mozley. New York: G. P. Putnam's Sons, 1929.
Philo, Judaeus. *On the Creation*. Vol. I of *Philo* in *The Loeb Classical Library*. Trans. F. H. Colson and G. H. Whitaker. 10 vols. New York: G. P. Putnam's Sons, 1929-1953.
Plato. *Symposium*. In *The Five Dialogues of Plato*. Trans. P. B. Shelley. London: J. H. Dent & Sons, 1929.
Plinius, Caecilius. *Letters*. In *The Loeb Classical Library*. Trans. William Melmoth. 2 vols. New York: The Macmillan Company, 1915.
Plinius, Gaius Secundus. *Natural History*. In *The Loeb Classical Library*. Trans. H. Rackham, W. H. S. Jones, and D. E. Eichholz. 10 vols. Cambridge, Massachusetts: Harvard University Press, 1938-1962.
Plotinus. *Enneada*. Trans. Stephen MacKenna. New York: Pantheon Press, 1957.
Plutarch. *Plutarch's Lives*. In *The Loeb Classical Library*. Trans. Bernadette Perrin. 11 vols. London: W. Heinemann, 1914-1927.

Sallustius Crispus, Gaius. *Sallust.* In *The Loeb Classical Library.* Trans. J. C. Rolfe. New York: G. P. Putnam's Sons, 1921.

Second Clement. Vol. VII of *The Ante-Nicene Fathers.* Trans. M. B. Riddle. 10 vols. Grand Rapids, Michigan: Wm. B. Eerdmans Company, 1951.

Seneca, Lucius. *Epistles.* In *The Loeb Classical Library.* Trans. R. M. Gummere. 3 vols. New York: G. P. Putnam's Sons, 1917-1925.

—. *On Benefits.* Trans. Aubrey Stewart. London: Bell, 1887.

Septuagint, The Old Testament in Greek. Edited by H. B. Swete. 3 vols. Cambridge: University Press, 1901-1905.

Sibylline Oracles. Trans. Milton S. Terry. New York: Eaton Mains, 1899.

Statius. *Silvae.* Vol. I of *Statius* in *The Loeb Classical Library.* Trans. J. H. Mozley. 2 vols. London: W. Heinemann, 1928.

Suetonius Tranquillus, Caius. *Suetonius.* In *The Loeb Classical Library.* Trans. H. C. Rolfe. 2 vols. New York: The Macmillan Company, 1914-1935.

Tacitus, Cornelius. *Annals.* In *The Loeb Classical Library.* Trans. John Jackson. 3 vols. London: The Macmillan Company, 1931-1937.

—. *Dialogus, Agricola, Germania.* In *The Loeb Classical Library.* Trans. Maurice Hutton and William Peterson. New York: The Macmillan Company, 1914.

Tatian. *Oration to the Greeks.* Vol. II of *The Ante-Nicene*

Fathers. Trans. Hope W. Hogg. 10 vols. Grand Rapids, Michigan: Wm. B. Eerdmans Company, 1951.

Tertullian. *Against Marcion*. Vol. III of *The Ante-Nicene Fathers*. Trans. F. Thelwall. 10 vols. Grand Rapids, Michigan: Wm. B. Eerdmans Company, 1951.

—. *Apology*. Vol. III of *The Ante-Nicene Fathers*. Trans. S. Thelwall. 10 vols. Grand Rapids, Michigan: Wm. B. Eerdmans Company, 1951.

—. *An Exhortation to Chastity*. Vol. XIII of *Ancient Christian Writers*. Edited by Johannes Quasten and Joseph C. Plumpe. Trans. W. P. Le Saint. Westminster, Maryland: The Newman Press, 1951.

—. *Monogamy*. Vol. XIII of *Ancient Christian Writers*. Edited by Johannes Quasten and Joseph C. Plumpe. Trans. W. P. Le Saint. Westminster, Maryland: The Newman Press, 1951.

—. *Of Patience*. Vol. III of *The Ante-Nicene Fathers*. Trans. S. Thelwall. 10 vols. Grand Rapids, Michigan: Wm. B. Eerdmans Company, 1951.

—. *On Baptism*. Vol. III of *The Ante-Nicene Fathers*. Trans. S. Thelwall. 10 vols. Grand Rapids, Michigan: Wm. B. Eerdmans Company, 1951.

—. *On Penitence*. Vol. XXVIII of *Ancient Christian Writers*. Edited by Johannes Quasten and W. J. Burghardt. Trans. W. P. Le Saint. Westminster, Maryland: The Newman Press, 1959.

—. *On Purity*. Vol. XXVIII of *Ancient Christian Writers*. Edited by Johannes Quasten and W. J. Burghardt.

Trans. W. P. Le Saint. Westminster, Maryland: The Newman Press, 1959.

—. *On the Dress of Virgins*. Vol. IV of *The Ante-Nicene Fathers*. Trans. S. Thelwall. 10 vols. Grand Rapids, Michigan: Wm. B. Eerdmans Company, 1951.

—. *The Prescription Against Heretics*. Vol. III of *The Ante-Nicene Fathers*. Trans. S. Thelwall. 10 vols. Grand Rapids, Michigan: Wm. B. Eerdmans Company, 1951.

—. *To His Wife*. Vol. XIII of *Ancient Christian Writers*. Edited by Johannes Quasten and Joseph Plumpe. Trans. W. P. Le Saint. Westminster, Maryland: The Newman Press, 1951.

—. *To the Nations*. Vol. III of *The Ante-Nicene Fathers*. Trans. S. Thelwall. 10 vols. Grand Rapids, Michigan: Wm. B. Eerdmans Company, 1951.

—. *Treatise on the Soul*. Vol. III of *The Ante-Nicene Fathers*. Trans. S. Thelwall. 10 vols. Grand Rapids, Michigan: Wm. B. Eerdmans Company, 1951.

Tibullus, Albius. *Tibullus*. Trans. M. Dart. London: T. Sharpe, 1720.

Ulpian, Domitius. *The Institutes of Gaius and Rules of Ulpian*. Trans. J. Muirhead. Edinburgh: T. & T. Clark, 1880.

Valerius Maximus. Trans. C. H. Peuchot and E. P. Allairs. Paris: Delalaum, 1822.

Virgil, Maro. *Aeneid*. In *The Loeb Classical Library*. Trans. A. S. Way. London: The Macmillan Company, 1950.

B. SECONDARY SOURCES

1. BOOKS

Abrahams, I. *Studies in Pharisaism and the Gospels.* Cambridge: University Press, 1917.

Allmen, J. J. von. *Marie et femmes d'après Saint Paul.* Paris: Delachaux and Niestle, 1951.

Amran, David. *The Jewish Law of Divorce.* Philadelphia: Edward Stern & Company, 1896.

Arndt, William, and Wilbur Gingrich. *A Greek-English Lexicon of the New Testament and Other Early Christian Literature.* Chicago: The University of Chicago Press, 1957.

Bailey, Sherwin. *Sexual Relations in Christian Thought.* New York: Harper & Brothers, 1959.

Bainton, Roland H. *What Christianity Says About Sex, Love, and Marriage.* New York: Association Press, 1957.

Baron, Salo. *A Social and Religious History of the Jews.* 7 vols. New York: Columbia University Press, 1952.

Becker, W. A. *Gallus; or Roman Scenes of the Times of Augustus.* Trans. Frederick Metcalfe. London: John W. Parker, 1844.

Bonsirven, Joseph. *Le Divorce dans le Nouveau Testament.* Paris: Desclee et Cie, 1948.

—. *Les enseignements de Jésus-Christ.* Paris: Beauchensne et ses fils, 1950.

Box, G. H., and Charles Gore. *Divorce in the New Testament.* London: S. P. C. K., 1921.

Bultmann, Rudolph. *Jesus and the Word.* Trans. Louise P. Smith and Erminie H. Lantero. New York: Charles Scribner's Sons, 1934.

Burrows, Millar. *The Basis of Israelite Marriage.* New Haven: American Oriental Society, 1938.

Carcopino, Jerome. *Daily Life in Ancient Rome.* Trans. E. O. Lorimer. New Haven: Yale University Press, 1941.

Chadwick, Henry, and J. E. L. Oulton. *Alexandrian Christianity.* Vol. II of *The Library of Christian Classics.* Edited by John Baillie. Philadelphia: The Westminster Press, 1952.

Charles, R. H. *Apocrypha and Pseudepigrapha of the Old Testament.* Oxford: Oxford University Press, 1913.

—. *Divorce and the Roman Law of Nullity.* Edinburgh: T. & T. Clark, 1927.

—. *The Teaching of the New Testament on Divorce.* London: William and Norgate, 1921.

Chase, F. N. *What Did Christ Teach About Divorce?* London: S. P. C. K., 1921.

Cirlot, Felix L. *Christ and Divorce.* Lexington, Kentucky: Trafton Publishing Company, 1945.

Cole, W. G. *Sex and Love in the Bible.* New York: Association Press, 1959.

Corbett, Percy. *The Roman Law of Marriage.* Oxford:

Clarendon Press, 1930.

Craig, Clarence T. *The First Epistle to the Corinthians.* In *The Interpreter's Bible.* New York: Abingdon-Cokesbury Press, 1953.

Cross, E. B. *The Hebrew Family.* Chicago: The University of Chicago Press, 1927.

Daube, David. *The New Testament and Rabbinic Judaism.* London: The University of London Press, 1956.

Dill, Samuel. *Roman Society from Nero to Marcus Aurelius.* London: The Macmillan Company, 1920.

Dodd, C. H. *Gospel and Law.* New York: Columbia University Press, 1951.

Döllinger, J. J. I. von. *First Ages of Christianity and the Church.* Trans. H. N. Oxenham. 2 vols. London: Gibblings and Company, 1866-1867.

Driver, S. R. *Deuteronomy.* In *The International Critical Commentary.* New York: Charles Scribner's Sons, 1895.

Easton, Burton Scott. *The Pastoral Epistles.* New York: Charles Scribner's Sons, 1947.

Edersheim, Alfred. *The Life and Times of Jesus the Messiah.* 2 vols. New York: Longmans, 1910.

Edmein, A. (ed.). *Le Mariage en Droit Canonique.* 2 vols. Paris: 1929.

Enslin, Morton Scott. *The Ethics of Paul.* New York: Harper and Brothers, 1930.

Epstein, Louis. *The Jewish Marriage Contract.* New York: Jewish Theological Seminary, 1927.

Findley, G. Vol. II in *Expositor's Greek New Testament.*

Edited by W. R. Nicoll. 5 vols. London: Hodder and Staughton, 1897-1910.

Finkelstein, Louis. *The Pharisees.* 2 vols. Philadelphia: The Jewish Publication Society, 1940.

Fowler, W. W. *Social Life at Rome in the Age of Cicero.* New York: The Macmillan Company, 1909.

Friedlander, L. *Moeurs romaines du règne d'Auguste à la fin des Antonins.* Trans. C. Vogel. 4 vols. Paris: C. Reinwald, 1865-1874.

Gasper, J. W. *Social Ideas in the Wisdom Literature.* Washington, D. C.: The Catholic University of America Press, 1947.

Gaster, T. H. (trans.). *The Dead Sea Scriptures.* Garden City, New York: Doubleday Anchor, 1957.

Gigot, Francis. *Christ's Teaching Concerning Divorce.* New York: Bensiger Brothers, 1912.

Gordon, C. H. *The World of the Old Testament.* New York: Harper and Brothers, 1958.

Gore, Charles. *The Question of Divorce.* New York: Charles Scribner's Sons, 1911.

Grosheide, F. W. *Commentary on the First Epistle to the Corinthians.* In *The New International Commentary on the New Testament.* Grand Rapids, Michigan: Wm. B. Eerdmans Company, 1953.

Hamilton, Edith. *The Roman Way to Western Civilization.* New York: The New American Library, 1957.

Harnack, Adolf. *The Expansion of Christianity in the First Three Centuries.* Trans. James Moffatt. 2 vols. New York: G. P. Putnam's Sons, 1904-1905.

Hefele, Charles. *A History of the Christian Councils.* Trans. Wm. R. Clark *et al.* 5 vols. Edinburgh: T. & T. Clark, 1871-1896.

Jacobson, I. *The Social Background of the Old Testament.* Cincinnati, Ohio: Hebrew Union College Press, 1947.

James, M. R. *The Apocryphal New Testament.* Oxford: Clarendon Press, 1924.

Johnson, Sherman E. *The Gospel According to Saint Matthew.* In *The Interpreter's Bible.* New York: Abingdon Press, 1951.

Juster, Jean. *Les Juifs dans l'Empire romain.* 2 vols. Paris: Librairie Paul Guethner, 1914.

Keil, C. F., and F. Delitzsch. *Pentateuch.* Trans. James Martin. 3 vols. Edinburgh: T. & T. Clark, 1857.

Kennett, R. H. *Ancient Hebrew Social Life and Customs as Indicated in Law, Narrative, and Metaphor.* London: British Academy, 1933.

Kiefer, Otto. *Sexual Life in Ancient Rome.* London: George Routledge & Sons, 1934.

Lacey, T. A. *Marriage in Church and State.* London: Robert Scott, 1912.

Lagrange, M. J. *Évangile selon saint Matthieu.* Paris: J. Gabalda et Fils, 1927.

Lecky, W. E. H. *History of European Morals from Augustus to Charlemagne.* New York: George Braziller, 1955.

Licht, Hans (pseud. Paul Brandt). *Sexual Life in Ancient Greece.* New York: Barnes & Noble, 1952.

Locke, Walter. *The Pastoral Epistles.* Edinburgh: T. & T.

Clarke, 1924.

Mace, David. *Hebrew Marriage.* New York: Philosophical Library, 1953.

Major, H. D. A., T. W. Manson, and C. J. Wright. *The Mission and Message of Jesus.* New York: E. P. Dutton, 1938.

Meyer, H. A. W. *Critical and Exegetical Handbook of the Gospel of Matthew.* Trans. Peter Christe. New York: Funk & Wagnalls, 1884.

Mielziner, M. *The Jewish Law of Marriage and Divorce.* New York: Bloch Printing Company, 1901.

Moffatt, James. *The First Epistle of Paul to the Corinthians.* London: Hodder & Stoughton, 1938.

Moore, G. F. *Judaism.* 3 vols. Cambridge: Harvard University Press, 1927-1930.

Murray, John. *Divorce.* Philadelphia: Orthodox Presbyterian Church, 1953.

O'Mahony, Patrick. *Catholics and Divorce.* New York: Thomas Nelson & Sons, 1958.

Ott, Anton. *Die Ehescheidung im Mattäus-Evangelium.* Würzburg: Rita-Verlag und -Druckerei, 1939.

Patai, Raphael. *Sex and Family in the Bible and the Middle East.* New York: Doubleday, 1959.

Pedersen, Johannes. *Israel.* Trans. A. Moller. 4 vols. London: Oxford University Press, 1926.

Piper, Otto. *The Christian Interpretation of Sex.* New York: Charles Scribner's Sons, 1953.

Pouratt, Pierre. *Christian Spiritualism.* Trans. W. H. Mitchell *el al.* 4 vols. Westminster, Maryland: Newman

Press, 1953.

Prat, Fernand. *Jesus Christ: His Life, His Teaching and His Work*. Trans. John J. Heenan. Milwaukee, Wisconsin: Bruce Publishing Company, 1950.

—. *The Theology of St. Paul*. Trans. John L. Stoddard. London: Burns, Oates and Washbourne, 1945.

Preisker, Herbert. *Christentum und Ehe in den ersten drei Jahrhunderten*. Berlin: Trowitsch & Sohn, 1927.

Robertson, A., and A. Plummer. *The First Epistle of St. Paul to the Corinthians*. In *The International Critical Commentary*. New York: Charles Scribner's Sons, 1911.

Rowley, H. H. *The Zadokite Fragments and the Dead Sea Scrolls*. Oxford: Basil Blackwell, 1952.

Ryder-Smith, Charles. *The Bible Doctrine of Womanhood*. London: The Epworth Press, 1923.

Simpson, E. K. *The Pastoral Epistles*. Grand Rapids, Michigan: Wm. B. Eerdmans Company, 1954.

Sohm, Rudolf. *The Institutes of Roman Law*. Trans. James Ledlie. Oxford: Clarendon Press, 1892.

Spicq, P. C. *Les Épitres Pastorales*. Paris: Librairie Lecofre, 1947.

Strack, H. L., and Paul Billerbeck. *Commentar zum Neuen Testament aus Talmud und Midrasch*. 4 vols. München: C. H. Beck, 1922-1928.

Thurian, Max. *Mariage et Célibat*. Paris: Delachaux et Niestle, 1955.

Toy, C. H. *Proverbs*. In *The International Critical Commentary*. New York: Charles Scribner's Sons, 1899.

Tyson, S. L. *The Teaching of Our Lord as to the Indissolubility of Marriage.* Sewanee, Tennessee: The University Press, 1909.

Watkins, O. D. *A History of Penance.* 2 vols. London: Longmans, Green Co., 1920.

—. *Holy Matrimony.* London: Rivington, Percival and Company, 1895.

Weiss, B. *Die vier Evangelien.* Leipzig: J. H. Hinrich, 1905.

Westermarck, Edward. *The History of Human Marriage.* 3 vols. London: The Macmillan Company, 1921.

Zahn, T. *Das Evangelium des Mattheas.* Leipzig: A. Deichertsche Verlagsbuchhandlung, 1922.

Zucrow, S. *Woman Slaves and the Ignorant in Rabbinic Literature.* Boston: The Stratford Company, 1932.

2. PERIODICALS AND MONOGRAPHS

Arendsen, J. P. "The Ante-Nicene Interpretation of the Sayings on Divorce," *The Journal of Theological Studies,* XX (1919).

Burrows, Millar. "Levirate Marriage in Israel," *Journal of Biblical Literature,* LIX (1940).

Campbell, Robert C. "Teaching of Paul Concerning Divorce," *Foundations,* VI (1963).

Colling, Oral. "Divorce in the New Testament," *The Gordon Review,* VII (1964).

Considine, T. P. "The Pauline Privilege," *Australasian*

Catholic Record, XL (1963).

Cooper, John C. "St. Paul's Evaluation of Women and Marriage," *Lutheran Quarterly*, XVI (1964).

Daube, David, "Concessions to Sinfulness in Jewish Law," *Journal of Jewish Studies*, X(1959).

Easton, Burton Scott. "Divorce in the New Testament," *Anglican Theological Review*, XXII (1940).

Epstein, Louis. "The Institution of Concubinage Among the Jews," *Proceedings of the American Academy for Jewish Research*, Vol. VI. Philadelphia: Jewish Publication Society (1935).

Frey, J. B. "La signification des termes *monandros* et *univira*," *Recherches de science religieuse*, XX (1930).

Gordis, Robert. "The Jewish Concept of Marriage," *Judaism*, II (1953).

Gordon, C. H. "The Status of Women Reflected in the Nuzi Tablets," *Zeitschrift für Assyriologie*, N. T. IX (1936).

Holsmeister, U. "Die Streitfrage über die Ehescheidungstexte bei Matthaus 5.32, 19.9," *Biblica*, XXXVI (1945).

Humbert, F. "La femme étrangère du livre des Proverbes," *Revue des études sémitiques*, XIII (1937).

Kornfeld, W. "L'adultère dans l'Orient antique," *Revue Biblique*, LVII (1950).

Lake, Kirsopp. "The Earliest Christian Teaching on Divorce," *Expositor*, 7th Series, X (1910).

O'Rourke, J. J. "A Note on an Exception: Mt. 5:32 (19.9) and I Cor. 7:12 Compared," *Heythrop Journal*, V (1964).

Paterson, John. "Divorce and Desertion in the Old Testament," *The Journal of Biblical Literature* (1927).

Smith, Harold. "Our Lord's Teaching on Divorce," *Expositor*, XVI (1919).

Vawter, Bruce. "The Divorce Clause in Mt. 5.32 and 19.9," *The Catholic Biblical Quarterly*, XVI (1954).

3. ENCYCLOPEDIA ARTICLES

Achelis, H. "Agapetae," *Encyclopedia of Religion and Ethics*. Edited by James Hastings. Vol. I. New York: Charles Scribner's Sons, 1922.

Arnou, R. "Plantonisme des Pères," *Dictionnaire de Théologie Catholique*. Edited by A. Vacant. Vol. XII, 2 Partie. Paris: Librairie Letouzey et Ané, 1934.

Foley, W. M. "Marriage (Christian)," *Encyclopedia of Religion and Ethics*. Edited by James Hastings. Vol. VIII. New York: Charles Scribner's Sons, 1922.

Greenwald, M. "Androgynes," *Jewish Encyclopedia*. Edited by Isidore Singer. Vol. I. New York: Funk and Wagnalls Company, 1901.

Hirsch, Emil. "Asceticism," *Jewish Encyclopedia*. Edited by Isidore Singer. Vol. I. New York: Funk and Wagnalls Company, 1901.

Kohler, K. "Essenes," *Jewish Encyclopedia*. Edited by Isidore Singer. Vol. IV. New York: Funk and Wagnalls Company, 1903.

Lehmkuhl, A. "Divorce," *The Catholic Encyclopedia*.

Edited by G. C. Herbermann. Vol. V. New York: Universal Knowledge Foundation, 1909.

Reid, J. S. "Asceticism (Roman)," *Encyclopedia of Religion and Ethics.* Edited by James Hastings. Vol. II. New York: Charles Scribner's Sons, 1922.

Rose, H. J. "Flamines," *The Oxford Classical Dictionary.* Edited by M. Gary, *et al.* Oxford: Clarendon Press, 1949.

Souarn, R. "Adultère," *Dictionnaire de Théologie Catholique.* Edited by A. Vacant. Vol. I, 1 Partie. Paris: Librairie Letouzey et Ané, 1903.

Thurston, Herbert. "Celibacy," *The Catholic Encyclopedia.* Edited by G. C. Herbermann. Vol. III. New York: Universal Knowledge Foundation, 1909.

INDEX OF SUBJECTS

INDEX OF NAMES